The Wade Collectors Handbook

Robert Prescott-Walker
E J Folkard
F J Salmon

Francis Joseph
ISBN 1-870703-61-8

Acknowledgements

I am very grateful for the help I have received from the staff of the Official International Wade Collectors Club, especially Adele Hall, in piecing together some of the more recent developments and products of Wade Ceramics Ltd.

I would also like to thank the staff at the various libraries and institutions that have helped me. In particular the staff at the Hanley Reference Library, most of whom have pushed trolleys laden with books into and out of their lift for me, not to mention innumerable fellow researchers, since 1980 often gaining little recognition for their services

Special thanks should also be made to Bill Buckley of the Potteries Antique Centre Ltd, Cobridge, Stoke-on-Trent, for his help in supplying some of the photographs and current market trends. With further assistance from Robin Reilly and G & G Collectables.

I would also like to thank the various former authors on the subject of Wade who have made great strides in opening up the past history of Wade Ceramics Ltd, particularly David Lee for his thoroughly well researched book.

Perhaps the most significant credit goes to the numerous collectors and dealers I have spoken to concerning the growing interest both in the UK and abroad over the last few years.

Last but not least, John Folkard who worked tirelessly on the listings and Frank Salmon who co-ordinated everything and put the photographs together with the help of Trevor Leak and Mark Oliver of Phillips.

Published in the UK by
Francis Joseph Publications
6 Southbrook Mews, London SE12 8LG
Telephone: 0181 318 9580

Typeset by E J Folkard Computer Services
199 Station Road, Crayford, Kent DA1 3QF

Printed in Great Britain by
Greenwich Press, London SE7 England

ISBN 1-870703-61-8

Contents

Introduction

Until very recently the precise history of the various Wade potteries and subsidiary businesses has seemingly been based on a few facts and family remembrances that have, over the years, been repeated, added to and enriched much in the manner of Chinese whispers until the story became accepted as gospel. Inevitably truth, facts and what were possibly meant as anecdotal information became merged to form what was believed and accepted to be the origins and story of the Wade family. No more. The true history of the Wade family and as a consequence the history of the pottery, has recently been uncovered by the researches of David Lee and Di Wade, no doubt aided by the researcher's luxury of insider information, bringing to task the myths and dispelling the cobwebs in one fell swoop. After obvious exhaustive and time consuming research, 'The Wade Dynasty', having taken the best part of ten years, according to the author, fairly bristles with a myriad of facts, dates and documentary evidence, based on the foundation of the family tree.

Portrait of Albert J Wade. Pottery and Glass Record, *March 1924.*

4

The history of Wade ceramics is initially a story of two separate businesses run independently, to an extent, by members of the same family, eventually coming together effectively in 1931, although not officially until 1935 when the Wade Potteries Ltd company was born, being floated on the stock exchange in the same year. When I say that the businesses were run independently this does not imply that there were two separate non- communicating Wade families, anything but, as sons and uncles involved on one side would quite happily go to work for the other business. One can but imagine the family evening meals and discussions that must have gone on afterwards revolving around the daily running and developments of both firms.

Both businesses, Wade Heath & Co. Ltd., and A. J. Wade Ltd., not only started within a few months of each other but also in the same part of Burslem, only separated by a road and a school, strengthening the notion of close family communication.

It would appear that much of the confusion surrounding the date previously associated with the founding of the Wade potteries is connected with the Hallen pottery, the latter ultimately being taken over by the George Wade & Son firm in 1905 who subsequently used the name of the Henry Hallen firm and the date it had supposedly been established, 1810, unaware of the fact that it it this should have been 1840, as part of the George Wade & Son's letterhead. Yes, that's right, a letterhead would appear to have been solely responsible for the inaccurate dating concerning the establishment of the Wade Potteries, seemingly perpetuated by, knowingly or not, the Wade family themselves and by various recent authors of Wade related books.

However, even this doesn't hold water. With only a modicum of research into the various monthly trade journals there are accurate references to the founding of the company, such as; 'The original business was founded in 1867 for the production of domestic pottery, but in 1890 the works were extended to include the manufacture of decorative glazed tiles for fire grates'. This information taken from a well highlighted article entitled 'Wade Potteries Limited' in the *Pottery and Glass Record*, November 1935 (pg.291) when the two companies joined. In the same publication, March 1924, there are several pages devoted to Albert Joseph Wade, under the feature title 'Potters of To-day', a regular monthly column, in which the date of the founding of the Wade firm, albeit a year out, is given as 1865. The same article suggests that the date for commencement of tile making was 1896, which is odd, to say the least, since the writer of the article was talking at the time to the one person who had been involved at the start of the tile making enterprise. Added to this is the fact that any highly commercially minded businessman, as Albert J. Wade was, would have known the value of implying that their company was at least as old and established, if not older, than it actually was.

Chronology

To show the progress of the two separate *Wade* businesses, the dates in **bold** are to indicate the development of the *John Wade & Co* pottery until the amalgamation and floatation in 1935 of the two firms.

1824 John Wade and Ann married. John's trade was a cabinet maker while his wife Ann ran the business side, also being involved in making upholstery based in the Nantwich area.

1830s Moved to Garden Street, Burslem. John still making furniture but also working for some of the local potteries to add to his income.

1840s The Wade family, Ann having had seven of her twelve children, moved to Globe Street, Burslem. John's furniture business and shop being in the same area of Dale Hall, Burslem.

1859 John Wade died, aged 57. Joseph, second son, already working full-time for a pottery, took over the business.

1866 John Wade together with his older brother Joseph bought cottages in Hall Street, with the help of their mother.

1867 Joseph changed the family business from furniture to one that he was familiar with, ceramics. Joseph with his brother John and a colleague named Myatt opened the first Wade pottery company, **Wade & Myatt**, having acquired some cottages (now forming part of the Wade car park) in Hall Street, behind the Hill Top Methodist Church. Here they made porcelain fittings for the textile industry.

1867 John Wade and partners James & Henry Colclough started the **Toy Works** in High Street, Burslem.

1868 **The Toy Works** renamed *John Wade & Co.*, where they manufactured affordable everyday teapots in the Rockingham style that where so popular during the period.

1869 *Wade & Co.* started to make ornamental figures which became a separate business run by *Wade & Colclough*. The following year Daniel Lingard joined the firm after the death of Henry Colclough.

1873 *Wade & Co.* changed name to *Wade & Colclough*.

1880 Myatt who had been having problems previously having to sell up to keep his family afloat, as had Joseph, left the business altogether.

1881 Joseph Wade died, aged 47. Joseph's son George returned to try and keep the company going. George was, however, not interested or qualified to carry out the task, spending the profits on drink. Eventually it was left to the uncles to rally round and save the firm.

Joseph's brother George, or George Senior as he was to become known, took it on.

1881   *Wade & Colclough* became *Wade, Colclough and Lingard* now producing a great variety of teapots in Rockingham, Stone and Jet ware, also making various other tea related items as well as match strikers, tobacco jars, ashtrays, coffee pots all in various decorative styles.

1882   Name of company changes to *Wade & Sons*, still making porcelain fittings for the textile industry. During the 1880s William and Albert joined their uncle John's firm *Wade & Co.*, by now established in High Street, Burslem, whilst George stayed at the declining *Wade & Sons.*

1886   George Henry Heath joins *Wade & Co.* as an office boy. Later he became a travelling salesman which was when he meet Albert J. Wade.

1887   John's partners split forming their own company, Colclough and Lingard, leaving John to run the business with his nephew William Wade and John Poxon, William's brother in law, the company reverting back to *Wade & Co.*

Wade & Co. introduced their first pottery mark **W & Co**, with a **B** underneath signifying Burslem. (Ref: Marks page 120)

1888   William designed and patented the 'Automatic Lock-Lid' teapot. In the same year John and William started a new venture, the manufacture of tiles.

1889   George bought *Wade & Sons* on 2nd December for £60 from Annie Marie Wade, Joseph's wife. Quickly introduced a harder porcelain for the manufacture of fittings for the textile industry, also branched out into gaslight and fire fittings.

1891   To accommodate the rapidly expanding tile business, which went by the name *J. & W. Wade & Co.*, the firm bought the High Street Pottery (formerly occupied by Heath & Greatbach) next to Wade & Co. and called it the **Flaxman Art Tile Works**

1892   George Wade Snr died aged 67.

1897   John Wade relinquishes control of *Wade & Sons* to his nephews William and Albert Joseph Wade.

1900   Firm's name changed to *George Wade*. Company prospered with growing housing developments both in Britain and abroad.

1901   *J. & W. Wade & Co.* part of the inaugural meeting of the **British Wall and Floor Tile Manufacturers' Association** on 14th January held at the Cobridge Social Club. This attempt to form an association to control prices and promote their own wares seems to have failed, as there appear to have been no further meetings beyond 1901.

1902 John Wade died, aged 66, leaving the Wade firms in the hands of his nephews William Wade, who concentrated on developing new designs, and Albert Joseph Wade who ran the business side of both *Wade & Co.* and the *J. & W. Wade* tile business, with a particular interest in advertising, later to prove an important part in the progress of the Wade firms.

1905 George buys out Hallen firm running both his own firm and the Hallens' as separate concerns until the following year.

1906 George establishes one large pottery – **The Manchester Pottery** – behind the Wade & Co. Flaxman works.

1907 After several year's involvement in local politics, becoming education spokesman, councillor George was made a JP for both Staffordshire and Stoke-on-Trent.

1910/13 William retires from the business and moves to Los Angeles, California. Albert J. Wade and George Henry Heath become senior directors of both *Wade & Co.* and *J. & W. Wade & Co.*

Albert J. Wade (*J. & W. Wade & Co.*) was one of the many members of the tile industry present at the inaugural meeting of 'The Glazed and Floor Tile Manufacturers' Association', 10th November, 1910, which paved the way for the British Tile Industry as we know it today.

1912 William Wade and George Wade Poxon establish the Wade Encaustic Tile Co. in California. Later taken over by Pelton Brothers.

1914 William Wade died in Los Angeles, California, returning from his daughter's funeral. Albert J. Wade becomes chairman of *Wade & Co.* and *J. & W. Wade & Co.* with George H. Heath Managing Director.

George Wade Poxon establishes another pottery under the name Furlong-Poxon Pottery, making art tiles and pottery.

1919 *George Wade* becomes *George Wade & Son* and the on 24th June 1919, *George Wade & Son Ltd.*

George Albert Wade, better known as Colonel Wade, returns from the war a hero and is made a partner in his father's firm.

1920 Fire at *J. & W. Wade & Co.* Sunday 1st August.

1922 Col G. A. Wade sets up The North Mill Company which processed quality raw materials for pottery making for his own pottery and later other potteries.

1927 George retires. His son Col. G. A. Wade having more or less run the pottery since 1918.

1927 *J. & W. Wade* and *Wade & Co.* become limited companies, the former becoming *A. J. Wade Ltd* and the latter *Wade, Heath & Co. Ltd.*

1929   Col. George employs **Jessie (Van) Hallen,** setting her up with her own department to make figures, animals, garden gnomes, floral items, etc.

1930   As part of Col. George Wade's improvements and expansion into the gift ware market he hires **Faust Lang** a gifted sculptor to design animals and birds.

1931   Col. G. A. Wade becomes a director of *Wade, Heath & Co. Ltd* and *A. J. Wade Ltd.*

1932   Albert J. Wade forced to retire due to ill health in November.

1933   Albert J. Wade dies aged 66 after a short illness.

1935   *Wade, Heath & Co. Ltd* and *A. J. Wade Ltd* became one company *Wade Potteries Limited* that was then floated on the stock market. Col. G. Wade as Chairman and George Heath as Managing Director. Annie F. Wade, Albert's wife, also became a senior director.

    Wade Heath started to make Royal Commemorative wares for the Silver Jubilee of King George V and Queen Mary.

1936   A new range called **Flaxman Ware** was introduced at the Wade Heath works along with a range of animals and some Walt Disney characters.

    Robert Barlow joins *Wade, Heath & Co. Ltd* about this time as a designer.

1937   George Henry Heath dies, aged 64.

    Col. G. Wade now running the *Wade Potteries* by himself moved the Wade Heath pottery to a site of it's own, The Royal Victoria Pottery, across the road from the other Wade buildings.

1938   George Wade JP dies on New Years Day aged 74.

    New showroom opened at *Wade, Heath & Co. Ltd.* The chief feature being a large mural of 'Snow White and the Seven Dwarfs' painted by **Robert Barlow**.

1939   Expansion plans were halted by the War, production being limited to either monochrome 'Utility' ware for the domestic market or decorative ware for export only.

1946   Col. G. Wade bought an old linen mill in Watson Street, Portadown, Northern Ireland, which he equipped for the manufacture of electrical porcelain and so started the Irish Wade connection.

1947   Col. G. Wade's son George Anthony J. Wade joined *George Wade & Son Ltd*, the following year becoming a director and then Joint Managing Director in 1949.

1950   *Wade Heath* becomes involved with a retail agency, **Reginald Corfield (Sales) Ltd,** the venture becoming known as *Wade Regicor*. This business was devoted to advertising wares used in bars and pubs by breweries and distilleries.

1950   The Wade Irish pottery becomes a private limited company, *Wade (Ulster) Ltd.*

Col. Wade starts experimental studio with **Colin Melbourne** as the modeller/designer.

1952   Introduction of the famous **Wade Whimsies,** a prototype horse being made by George Anthony J. Wade, better known as Tony.

1953   The first set of five **Wade Whimsies** was shown, complete with an especially designed box, at the British Industries Fair and made a great hit with many buyers, especially those abroad.

1954   **Mr W. K. Harper** was employed as modeller and designer of the lucrative **Wade Whimsies,** being responsible almost all the designs of the sets produced during the 1950s and early 1960s, amongst many other designs.

1955   Col. G. Wade was knighted for his political services.

1956   A fire at *Wade (Ulster) Ltd* almost destroyed the business, but it was up and running again shortly after and rebuilding completed by 1958.

1958   *Wade Potteries Limited* took over *George Wade & Sons Ltd,* together with *Wade (Ireland) Ltd* that had for so long been outside the publicly owned Wade Potteries. All the Wade companies now being under one roof, so to speak.

1959   Demand for tiles and tiled fireplaces fell resulting in *A. J. Wade Ltd* reducing the work force considerably. By 1962 only specialist low volume tiles were being made, this business being reduced still further until in 1970 *A. J. Wade Ltd* ceased to exist.

1964   *Wade Potteries Ltd* took over William Kent (Porcelains) Ltd and tooled up solely for the manufacture of electrical porcelains and fittings for the electronic industry.

1965   Giftware, including many of the Whimsey sets, were cut by Col. George returning to industrial ceramics and advertising wares.

1966   *Wade (Ulster) Ltd* changed it's name to *Wade (Ireland) Ltd,* making gift ware and Whimsies until 1986.

1969   *Wade* launched *Wade (PDM) Limited,* having split with Reginald Corfield. This new Wade Point-of-Sale, Design and Marketing company was initially based in Purley, Surrey until in 1989 it relocated to The Royal Victoria Pottery.

1970   *A. J. Wade Ltd* ceased operations.

1971   Tony Wade becomes chairman of *Wade Potteries Ltd* after his father retires.

Ken Holmes and **Alan Maslankowski** both left Royal Doulton to join Wade. Ken Holmes as a blockmaker, later becoming head modeller for George Wade & Son Ltd in the 1980s. Alan Maslankowski as a designer is responsible for both the 'Survival' and 'Connoisseur' series.

1975   Govencroft Potteries Ltd taken over. This lasted until 1981.

1984   *Wade Potteries Ltd* moves into space technology opening an aerospace division making nose-cones for rockets and later developed a ceramic coated alloy together with other companies.

1985   **Barbara Cookson** joins Wade Ceramics as designer at the Royal Victoria Works.

1987   Tony Wade died of leukaemia aged 63

1988   **Judith Wooten** joins Wade as a ceramic designer.

1990   *Wade Potteries Ltd* was taken over by *Beauford plc* and ceased to be an independent company. The name changed to *Wade Ceramics Ltd*

        Wade (Ireland) Ltd became *Seagoe Ceramics Ltd*, making advanced engineering ceramics, tableware and one or two lines of gift ware.

1992   *Wade (Ireland) Ltd* wound up, the machinery was transferred to the Burslem site, Seagoe now concentrating on advanced ceramic processes and technologies, with large financial resources committed to new building projects in Portadown.

1994   *Wade Ceramic Fibers*, Inc established in Winchester, Kentucky, America, as the company's US subsidiary. The new state-of-the-art factory expands the international reputation and leadership of Wade in the market of fuel-effect components with the development and manufacture of ceramic fibre firelogs and other fibre based products for the gas fireplace and stove markets. Future projected markets are hoped to include industrial engineered ceramics.

        The Official International Wade Collector Club was launched during this year with the first magazine out in September just in time for the first **UK Wade Collectors Fair** held on 24th September.

1995   Wade purchase A. G. Hackney & Co. Ltd from G.E.C. This site, directly opposite the Wade Royal Victoria Pottery and the Manchester Pottery, has now been re-named the Wade Royal Works and adds greatly to Wades industrial ceramic market.

1996   The **first US Wade Fair** held at the Red Lion Hotel, Seattle Airport, in July. The fair was organised by The International Association of Jim Beam Bottle & Speciality Collectors Club.

The History – Teapots and Creels

The first Wade pottery venture was effectively started in 1866 with the purchase of some cottages in Hall street, Burslem, by Joseph and John Wade, together with a business partner named Myatt. The following year, 1867, Wade & Myatt were open for business making porcelain fittings for the textile industry, such as creel steps and shuttle eyes, in direct competition with the already well established Henry Hallen pottery (founded in 1840).

This embryonic development of the Wade Potteries had come about as a result of the death, in 1859, of Joseph and John's father John Wade. The main family business until this time had been furniture making with Ann, John Wade's wife, running the shop and making her own mattresses and embroidered cushions. Joseph, who had been working for one of the local potteries, as had his father occasionally, tried to keep the furniture business going but soon realised that he was not a cabinet maker and that a change of direction was needed. This transition to the making of pottery should now be recognised as being the true date of the founding of the Wade Potteries, namely 1867.

In the same year John Wade, leaving his older brother Joseph and Myatt to run the Wade & Myatt pottery, went into partnership with James and Henry Colclough taking over what was called the Toy Works in the High Street of Burslem. By 1868 they had opened John Wade & Co. where they manufactured affordable everyday teapots, in the popular Rockingham style. By 1870 the pottery had been joined by Daniel Lingard, as a result of the death of Henry Colclough, shortly after which the firm changed its name to Wade and Colclough. They had by this time started to make ornamental figures much in the same vein as the traditional Staffordshire flatbacks, the figures given as fairground prizes and sold on local market stalls.

Meanwhile the Wade & Myatt business had been slowly developing until the 1880s when firstly Myatt pulled out of the pottery, having financial problems, followed by the death of Joseph Wade the following year. Immediately Joseph's son George, who had married the year before and moved to Wolstanton, returned to try and keep the company going. This proved to be too much for George who did not have the knowledge or experience needed to run a pottery, instead spending any profits on rich living. Before long the business was in a very poor state.

Saving the firm was left to Joseph's brother George, or George Senior as he was to become known, who had plenty of pottery experience, starting as a potters' apprentice at the age of 14, eventually becoming a thrower, which was, and in many ways is still, regarded as being one of the best and most highly regarded jobs in a pot bank. The first thing George Snr. did, in 1882, was to change the name to Wade & Sons, the latter referring to Joseph's sons, George, William and Frederick with Joseph's brother John still having an interest. For the next eight years George Snr. and his nephews struggled to keep the company going until George senior's son, George, returned to the Potteries.

Shortly after George Snr. had launched his rescue attempt of the Wade and Sons firm, his own sons, William and Albert Joseph, went to work with John Wade at what was by that time called the firm of Wade, Colclough and Lingard. Teapots and figures were no longer the only items made by this firm; they had extended the range of products to include coffee pots and teapot stands, together with other related tea wares, as well as tobacco jars, match strikers and sundry tobacco related items. William and Albert Joseph joined their uncle John, along with William's brother-in-law, John Poxon, during 1887, shortly after James Colclough and Daniel Lingard went on their own setting up another teapot manufacturer in Tunstall. It was also during this period that Wade & Co. took on a new office boy who was to play an important role in the company later, namely George Henry Heath.

Following the arrival of William and Albert Joseph, John Wade again changed the name of the pottery this time reverting back to Wade & Co. In the same year Albert Joseph introduced marks to Wade & Co. pottery. The first mark being W & Co., with a B underneath indicating that the item had been made in Burslem. The use of the initial letter of the town of manufacture was a well-established and recognised form of distinguishing potteries which used the same initials in their marks. Details of subsequent marks can be seen in a later chapter.

Of the two brothers, Albert Joseph and William, it was the latter who was initially to shine, developing various new methods of making and decorating teapots, tiles, even firing kilns, taking out some 18 patents. Albert Joseph Wade started to learn how to run the business also acting as a travelling salesman or promoter of the company. Over the following months Albert soon realised the necessity and importance of promotion through advertising, something that was subsequently to play a significant role from the 1950s.

Demand for Tiles

In 1888 with the teapot and sundries side of the business becoming more and more successful John and William started a new venture making tiles. This was also to prove a lucrative market. The new business, which went under the title of J. & W. Wade & Co. was established in new premises purchased next to the Wade & Co. buildings (formerly occupied by Heath & Greatbach) and was called the Flaxman Art Tile Works (now part of the Wade factory shop).

Wades were not alone in establishing a tile works at the end of the nineteenth century; they were one of many such firms all clamouring for business during the building boom of the period. There was a rapid development of civic building with hotels, shops, Inns and public houses, but above all numerous new hospitals, being built throughout the country as well as abroad. It was the beginning of an almost hysterical attitude towards cleanliness and hygiene, spurred on by outbreaks of various wide spread contagious illnesses and diseases. Builders often incorporated rooms in the new developments, particularly hospitals, with entire walls, floors and ceilings covered with tiling, the glazed ceramic surfaces being very easy to wash and therefore hygienic. Such was the demand for tiles both nationwide and internationally that firms sprung up just to cash in on the boom. Other potteries, much in the same vein as Wade, who had begun making tiles as a sideline to their main business, soon devoted an entire premises to tile manufacture.

It was entirely due to the ceaseless demand for tiles that one of the most important and far reaching technological developments concerning the mass-production of tiles came about. This was in fact the last and most significant break through, after a long line of technological improvements aimed at the manufacture of mass-production wares, which was to affect not just the tile industry, for which it had initially been invented, but the whole production of ceramic wares in the Potteries along with other major pottery centres throughout the world. The break through was developed by Conrad Gustave D'huc Dressler with the 'Dressler Tunnel Oven'. By 1905 Conrad Dressler had built the first 125 foot long tunnel oven which he fired continuously for six months firing some three million tiles. Today tunnel ovens are the main form of firing, with the major tile manufacturers producing on one site over three million tiles in a month.

On the 14th January, 1901, J. & W. Wade & Co was one of the tile companies that met at the inaugural meeting of *The British Wall and Floor Tile Manufacturers' Association*, held at the Cobridge Social Club. The aim of the association was to try and regulate the price of tiles as well as promote the wares of its members. However, there seemed to be little enthusiasm for other members to join or indeed amongst its own members, the association meeting for the last time on 14th May. It was 1910 that a serious attempt was made again to form an association. On 23rd November at the North Stafford Hotel, A. J. Wade (J. & W. Wade & Co) was one of eighteen representatives from the tile industry, with six other firms absent, who attended the inaugural meeting of *The Glazed and Floor Tile Manufacturers' Association*. Albert Wade appeared standing in the back row of a group photograph along with the other representatives that attended, to commemorate the event. Over the years the association adopted various policies on pricing, wages, promotion of members' wares, standardisation of tile sizes, foreign competition and tendering for government and industrial contracts, working wherever possible for the mutual benefit and support of the members. It was this Association that was to form the foundation for todays *British Ceramic Tile Council*.

Until the 1920s decorative tiles were largely restricted in the average house to fireplace surrounds, the porch and in the back of wash stands, only occasionally being used in other pieces of furniture. It was in this area that the new J & W. Wade & Co. tile venture was initially to specialise, producing tiles in a wide range of decorative styles showing influences of Persian tiles, popular during the turn of the century, as well as Etruscan and Antique, together with various mottled and streaked colour glaze combinations. The company often received a great deal of praise for their 'Persian Craquelle' glaze effect, which could be produced in a wide variety of high quality colours. The glaze effects ranged from a brilliant gloss enamel through to what was known as an 'Eggshell' effect (see colour illustration). Later into the 1920s they started to employ transfer prints to form the outline of the pattern that would then be filled with coloured enamels and then in the 1930s full colour scenes of nursery rhymes were used on a dull or matt coloured glaze. By this time Wade's were making up complete fireplace surrounds at their works, which were supplied to their own retailers, as well as supplying boxed separates to the building trade.

Such was their reputation, and thanks to the travelling salesman, Mr Albert J. Wade himself, Wade tiles have found their way into a church for the Saint Francis Brotherhood, in Buenos Ayres, Princess Mary's town house, Chesterfield House and Goldsborough House, not to mention some very large commissions for Salisbury House in London, various underground stations in London as well as numerous provincial Town Halls, hospitals, etc.

All this time, as the tile business was rapidly developing, demand and sales of their teapots was also expanding. New shapes and styles of decoration were constantly being introduced, keeping pace with rapidly fluctuating tastes and fashions. The years spanning the turn of the century were for many a time of increased wealth, largely due to economic growth, with rapidly expanding commercial markets abroad and a huge increase in the establishment of new business eager to cash in on markets in South Africa, the United States, Canada, South America, Australia and Europe. The growth of new money in the upper and middle classes in Britain, along with the development of new business and the expansion of others, meant that the prosperity and prospects of those carrying out the labour and making also increased, with a commensurate rise in spending power.

It was not until the 1960s that the specific demand for British tiles started to wane following an influx of cheaper continental tiles, together with the start of the DIY market, which brought a restructuring of the tile industry, ending in almost all the tile manufacturers in Stoke-on-Trent being owned by one company, the rest closing down.

A. J. Wade Ltd continued to be a member of the British Ceramic Tile Council, along with the National Fireplace Manufacturers' Association that was formed later, even though tile production was greatly affected by a restructuring in the late 1950s. During the 1960s the tile department was reduced to buying in blanks from H. & R. Johnson that were then decorated and sold under the H. & R. Johnson 'Cristal' brand. One such set of tiles being the 'Kitchen Series No: 1', sold under the 'Gems – Ceramic Tile Insets' label, which shows six tile designs by Rhys & Jean Powell of stylised fruit and bowls of fruit. Other tiles with stylised faces are also known to have been executed by Rhys & Jean Powell.

Even these one-off series of designs could not save the tile department. Whether because of domestic or foreign competition, by 1970 the name of A. J. Wade Ltd disappeared from the various association lists as tile production finally ceased.

*Three models made exclusively for UK Fairs: **Spaniel** in 1994 in a limited edition of 1000, originally sold for £12.50/$25.00 but now commands a price tag of £65/$130. **Timid Mouse** issued in 1996 in a limited edition of 1750 now fetches £35/$70 each compared with the original selling price of £16/$30. Both models are 4 inches in size.*

Business Expansion

At the other family firm, Wade & Sons, still making their porcelain fittings for the textile industry, little had altered, but change was in the wings. George Wade Snr. was in semi-retirement in the mid 1880s, acting as a supervisor of the firm until his third son, George, returned from his university studies and a subsequent position as a school master in Leicestershire, in 1888/89.

Almost as soon as George had returned to the potteries with a new family of his own, he purchased the Wade & Sons business for £60 paid over a period of time to Anne Marie Wade, wife of Joseph Wade. His father, having struggled for many years to keep the business afloat, saw his son, who was later to become a Justice of the Peace, take control in 1889 and then died three years later in 1892, aged 67.

George soon took a firm hold of the company introducing a new harder porcelain body for the manufacture of the textile industry fitments, thereby regaining lost former customers and gaining others at the expense of the competition. He then started to introduce new product ranges for the gas industry and later, with the introduction of electricity, he supplied switches, knobs, junction boxes, fuse holders, housing of heating elements and many other components. It was not long before Wade & Sons was once more a highly competitive firm thanks largely once again to the new money and huge housing boom that was evident around the turn of the century, along with the increased growth and similar housing boom in foreign countries.

By 1900, having re-established the firm amongst his fellow competitors, George once again changed the name of the firm, to George Wade. Such was the success of the firm that by 1905 George Wade was able to buy out the Henry Hallen pottery, for so long a thorn in their side. Following this take over George was able to buy more land and in 1906 established the Manchester Pottery, behind the Wade & Co. Flaxman Works. Not content with that he set up another business, 'The Chromo Transfer and Potters' Supply Co.', which, as the title implies, offered colour transfers and colours for decorating, along with materials for making pottery and china.

Throughout this time George found time to become very involved in County politics becoming Chairman of the old Burslem School Board (later the Burslem Education Committee), secretary of the Newcastle-under-Lyme Liberal Association, and also becoming very involved in the debate over the federation of the six towns which ultimately came to fruition in 1910 under the title 'Stoke-on Trent'. In 1907 he became a Justice of the Peace and might at one stage have stood for Parliament, but declined.

In the midst of this highly successful period for both the Wade firms, John Wade, aged 61, decided to retire in 1897, leaving his nephews William and Albert Joseph in charge of Wade & Co. and J. & W. Wade & Co. Only five years after his retirement John Wade died in November 1902, with full control of the firm passed to William and Albert.

John Wade and his nephews William and Albert Joseph, realising the virtue of expanding the business, used the profits of the companies to bring in the latest machines related to the manufacture of the various wares, including new kilns, and increased the number of workers, thereby increasing output and the range of products, along with an improvement in the quality of wares.

Another highly successful tool employed by Wade & Co., one that was to become highly significant after the second war, afforded by increased profits, was advertising. The use of advertising to promote increased sales was something that Albert Joseph Wade was especially aware of and keen to develop. Having been established for many years and with healthy profits, Wades' had an advantage over all the newly established firms making similar wares for the first time and unable to afford the luxuries an advertising campaign. Albert embarked on a wide advertising programme within the various specialist monthly trade journals, related to ceramics and building, and the newly published home decorating magazines, often using full page adverts, with adverts having photographs of their latest designs. The accompanying promotional script was used to leave the reader in no doubt about the quality, global sales, variety and competitiveness of their wares, along with the virtues and years of experience of such a well established traditional firm.

By now Wade tiles had found their way into numerous hospitals, the London Underground, various hotels, both in Britain and abroad, and numerous other buildings, not to mention thousands of houses. Much of the success of both Wade & Co and J. & W. Wade & Co. was due to the devotion and commercial awareness of Albert J. Wade who forsook, unlike some of his predecessors, any high profile involvement in local politics and such like, instead preferring to spend time on the demands of running and developing a successful business. What little time remained he gave to the Wesleyan church and Newcastle Male Voice Choir. In relation to his commercial concerns he was president or chairman of the Jet and Rockingham Manufacturers' Association for sixteen years which he relinquished at the end of 1923.

In his unceasing efforts to promote and develop the business Albert was a frequent traveller abroad, making the most of the rapidly improving transport networks during the early part of this century, finding new buyers all over the world. It must be remembered that travel then was still a very lengthy, time consuming business. Albert at one time would appear to have spent six months in California where by this time his brother William had emigrated in about 1910/11. William was waiting in Los Angeles for his nephew George Wade Poxon, (possibly the son of Harriet Wade, sister to William and Albert, who married a Poxon) who had been involved in pottery making in Stoke for several years, so that they could set up a tile making business. By 1912 they had started the Wade Encaustic Tile Company, which was bought by the Pelton Brothers in 1915, subsequently purchased by the American Encaustic Tiling Company in 1917. It was after the untimely and tragic death of William Wade in an automobile accident returning from the funeral of his daughter that George Wade Poxon started another pottery making both tiles and art pottery, under the name Furlong-Poxon Pottery. One can only speculate as to the input or advice that Albert might have given his brother during his stay.

After the death of William Wade, Albert became chairman of both Wade & Co. and J. & W. Wade & Co., with George Henry Heath, the latter formerly joint senior director of the two companies with Albert, following William's departure to California, now becoming managing director. One of the first major problems the new team had to deal with was a large fire on 1st August 1920 during the traditional wake's weeks, better known as the potters' holidays. The fire was discovered in the early afternoon with the roof of the saggar house ablaze, the fire having spread from a nearby oven. Even though the fire brigade arrived within minutes the fire quickly spread to the drying room and warehouse. After an hour the fire was brought under control, but this did not stop considerable damage to the premises.

It did not take long for the damage to be repaired and full production to be restored, Wade's teapots still showing the lead to fellow manufacturers during the 1920s by continually introducing new teapot shapes and surface pattern designs to keep ahead of the field. One such design became known as the 'Cosy Set', in which the teapot and water jug were specially designed, by being almost the same size, to fit into a small tray or stand so that they were unable to move or slip off, both pieces then being covered with a cosy, hence the title. This set proved to be very popular, being copied by several other manufacturers, which in itself was high praise. By 1927 the tile and teapot businesses were doing so well that they became private limited companies, J. & W. Wade & Co. became A. J. Wade Ltd. and later in the same year Wade & Co. changed to Wade, Heath & Co. Ltd. Wade Heath, as it became known, ever responsive to changes in popular demand, introduced several new ranges and developed a wide selection of new shapes including vases with arrangers, wall chargers, flower bowls and jugs (pitchers), and boxes and covers, to name but a few. Along with the new shapes came new surface patterns and decorative processes, indicative of the growing experimental approach seen in many potteries between the wars. Brightly coloured hand-painted stylised, abstract and natural floral designs were all the rage, together with mottled and streaked decorative colour effects, the latter sold under the name 'Orcadia Ware'. The new abstract shapes often had very little correlation to the surface pattern design, but that did not seem to matter as long as the effect was modern, colourful, different from anything that had gone before, and above all else, affordable. Low-relief and high-relief moulded landscapes, garden scenes, flowers, animals and birds, etc, were also very popular, in many instances carrying on throughout the 1930s and into the 1940s.

By this time George Wade Snr. was nearing retirement, leaving his son George Albert Wade to run the George Wade pottery and the Chromo Transfer & Potters' Supplies businesses. After the war Major George A. Wade returned, the company changing its name to George Wade & Son, followed a year later in 1919, when the company took on private limited status, to George Wade & Son Ltd. Profits had been growing steadily along with the ever growing demand for gas and electricity nationally and internationally. With plenty of capital Major Wade started a new business in 1922 called The North Road Mill Company supplying all the raw materials needed by Major Wade, at the same time ensuring high quality and consistency. Later the business expanded, supplying various other potteries, ultimately leading to the opening of another mill in 1932.

The 1920s whilst being boom years for many in the potteries were also fraught with frustration over lost orders due to cheaper foreign products and strikes in the mining industry which had a devastating effect on fuel supplies for ceramic manufacturers, many having to close down for months only occasionally resuming work on a much reduced scale. Major Wade was an important figure in the midst of this turbulent time, often loudly voicing his opinions on what should be done to prevent the importation of cheap products and on the coal shortages. Major Wade, seemingly alone, advocated a switch to oil-firing, following lengthy experiments resulting in the conversion of all his own kilns to this new method of firing. He wrote papers and made speeches for the local trade detailing exactly what he had done and outlined the numerous advantages that could be had. These included cleaner burning fuel, greater accuracy of temperature control, a reduction in firing time, as well as a reduced loss of ware from the kiln and a reduced cooling time which consequently improved overall economy. Other advantages were to the environment, storage of the fuel supply being easier and a complete lack of

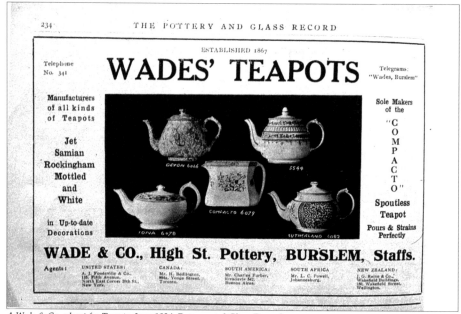

A Wade & Co. advert for Teapots, June 1924, Pottery and Glass Record

smoke that was normally so detrimental to the health of all the inhabitants of the Potteries. It is worth noting that the Pottery Trade press made quite a point of the fact that Major Wade had not kept the results of his experiments to himself, such was the largess of the man, offering the fruits of his labours to both competitors and non-competitors alike, two or three firms immediately converting to oil-firing as a result, with many more to follow.

Just by way of an aside a certain William Staite Murray, a former student of Bernard Leach and by 1926 a highly regarded studio potter himself, wrote to the *Times* having read of the changes to oil-firing that had recently been going on in the Potteries, supporting the substitution of oil for coal saying that he had himself undertaken the use of oil-firing in 1923, following many years of experimentation. The manner of the letter, typical of the rivalry between Studio Potters and Industry, seems one of surprise that the ceramics industry had taken so long to realise the advantages of oil-firing. A bit of one-up manship.

On the subject of cheap foreign imports Major Wade, having had first hand experience losing a lucrative and much needed order, again made his views extremely public, advocating that there should be legislation to prevent such foreign firms, who paid their workers half that of the British firms, from stopping 'a Britisher selling his own goods to his own people'. Such sentiments reflected those of many pottery owners, although others reserved their views for the various private committee meetings on the subject.

Clay models from the Children of the World series. The set consists of Japanese Girl (pictured on page 84), Spanish Girl, Indian Boy and Mexican Boy. Prices as yet have not been announced.

Enter the Designers

Towards the end of the 1920s Major Wade was looking to increase the public profile of his company, along the lines of that for so long associated with the other half of the Wade family, and he decided to employ a designers. To achieve this he employed Jessie Hallen, perhaps better known as Jessie Van Hallen, in 1929, setting up a new design department at the Manchester pottery, which Jessie was in charge of and from where there soon started to appear a wealth of figurines, garden gnomes, models of animals and the like.

Jessie's formative training was at the Burslem School of Art, where she was later to return to concentrate on pottery after studying life drawing in London. Perhaps the most important influence on her work, as with so many students studying modelling in the Burslem School of Art during this period, would have been William Ruscoe, the modelling teacher. It was his sense of flair, expression, lyricism and exaggeration of form that can often be seen to form the basis of many of his students' work. One or two of Jessie's early figures bare a striking resemblance to the work of her teacher. Jessie then developed her own flamboyant, humoresque, dancing style of figurines, probably influenced by the more sophisticated dancing figurines of continental potteries such as Royal Dux, Goldscheider and Katzhutte amongst others. Jessie, with her own typically British styling, gained admiration from her own countrymen, if only for a relatively short period. Her figures were noted in the trade press for 1935 as being 'full of vigour and (having) the suggestion of action'. In the same commentary 'Christina, a girl dog-trainer', is noted as being the latest figure in a line of 42 such figures, including animals. Part of the success of these figures, again noted at the time, was 'their bright colouring, "Scintillite" finish and popular prices'. Keeping the prices below those of Royal Doulton figurines and other firms was a deliberate policy that was achieved by the use of what was called a 'Scintillite' finish which meant there was no need for the added expense of a glaze firing. The Scintillite coating, patented by Wade, involved spraying a thin layer of cellulose acetate, an early form of plastic, over the surface of the figures which made the colours below brighter and richer, although the cellulose was never actually clear, having an ivory/yellow cast. This layer of cellulose proved to be not very durable, the yellow hue becoming stronger and more noticeable over the months and if the figures were placed on window sills or in direct sunlight the cellulose would rapidly flake and peel off. The same effect would also occur if the figures were placed in damp surroundings, the low-fired body itself absorbing moisture.

Jessie's arrival at the Manchester pottery was somewhat unfortunately timed as it coincided with the 1929 Wall Street crash and subsequent slump in European stock markets, followed by several years of economic uncertainty, which would undoubtedly have affected potential sales. However, even in such a depressed climate the figurines did sell well, Jessie and her paintresses frequently giving demonstrations throughout the country, as did a few other enterprising pottery firms. This was no doubt due to their perhaps most endearing feature, in that they reflected the gaiety and spirit of the era in which they were made, albeit late on.

The success and popularity of Jessie's figures was noted by a few other pottery manufactuers. Just prior to the Second World War almost identical figures were being made at the Howard Pottery Co. Ltd., under the Brentleigh Ware trade name and being openly advertised in 1944.

As part of his new drive to improve the public profile of the company George Wade then employed another modeller, Faust Lang, a well respected sculptor, to model animals and birds. Faust Lang's work until this time had mostly been concerned with modelling animals and birds as wooden sculptures, therefore making the transition to working with such a malleable material as clay a difficult one. It would appear that the transition was too difficult, Faust continuing to develop his initial prototypes in wood. The resultant high-fired glazed porcelain animals and birds sometimes owe much to the models of the Royal Copenhagen pottery in initial appearance with sometimes a very lithe and sleek look combined with quite a subtle palette. On other occasions some of his work, especially the models of birds with their bright colours seem rather brash, stiff and awkward, probably the effect of modelling the figures in wood. In any event the world record for a piece of Wade sold at auction is at present held by a Faust Lang model 'Ermine on a Rock' which sold for just over £1,700.

Another designer working for Wades during the 1930s was Robert Barlow, again a former student of the Burslem School of Art. Mr Barlow seems to have been taken on between 1935-36, certainly by 1938 he was being referred to as one 'of the firm's (two) principle designers' (the other being Jessie Van Hallen) in an article concerning the opening of the new Wade, Heath & Co. showroom for which he executed a large mural painting.

It was during this period just prior to the war that some significant changes occurred to both of the Wade family firms that formed the foundations of the present Wade Potteries company.

Merging of the Companies

In 1931 George Wade, following the failing health of Albert Joseph Wade, became a director of A. J.Wade Ltd. as well as Wade, Heath & Co. Ltd. Albert, who finally had to retire completely towards the end of the following year, died after a short illness in January 1933. George Wade and George Heath, following the death of Albert decided to join the two Wade firms which would then be floated on the stock exchange. Wade Potteries Limited was launched on 29th October 1935 with George Wade as Chairman and George Heath as Managing Director, also with Annie F. Wade, Albert's wife, as a senior director. A report in the monthly Pottery and Glass Record mentions that the North Road Mill Company was also included and that the combined profits for the three in 1934 were £17,286. Subscription lists for the shares were reported as being heavily over subscribed.

With the new company now well and truly underway new ranges and markets were opened up. Commemorative ware was one of the first new avenues to be embarked upon firstly for the Silver Jubilee of King George V and Queen Mary and subsequently for every Royal birth, marriage, coronation, etc. Along with numerous other pottery firms such as Myott's, A. J. Woods, Weatherby, Brentleigh and Keele Street Pottery amongst others, Wade Potteries launched their Flaxman Ware range, the shapes and decoration of which can only be described as too full of life, imagination, vitality and colour. It seemed that almost anything would do, from unusual, even zany, moulded castle turret shaped vases with budgerigars somewhat incongruously perched on handles, to conical shaped jugs with anything from an angular handle to several looping handles asymmetrically placed on either side.

Other items of note were the Walt Disney characters on various items, most notably the Donald Duck teapot (see Illustration), a Wade and teapot collectors' favourite.

Following the death in 1937 of George Henry Heath, at the age of 64, and then a year later the death of his father George, Major George Wade took on full responsibility for running the Wade Potteries, moving the main site across to his own works at the Royal Victoria Pottery. However, before any plans or alterations could be put into operation the Second World War interrupted proceedings. There was, however, one thing that the Major was able to do before hostilities were embarked upon and that was to open a new factory showroom at the Wade, Heath & Co. works, which opened on 14th November, as reported in the trade press. The chief feature of this colourful showroom, which received praise for the brilliancy of the lighting scheme, was a large hand painted mural executed in his spare time by Mr R. Barlow, previously mentioned as one of the two chief designers. The mural depicted a scene from 'Snow White and the Seven Dwarfs', for which Mr Barlow received from Major Wade a posy bowl of anemones made in china in appreciation of his talented work. By this time Wades were producing a set of the Disney Snow White characters designed by Jessie Van Hallen. However war brought a change in production and use of buildings, Wade's turnover during the War effort was confined to making plain white 'utility' wares and electrical goods with other parts of the works being used as storage facilities. George himself was promoted to the rank of Colonel and put in charge of the Birkenhead Garrison in 1940.

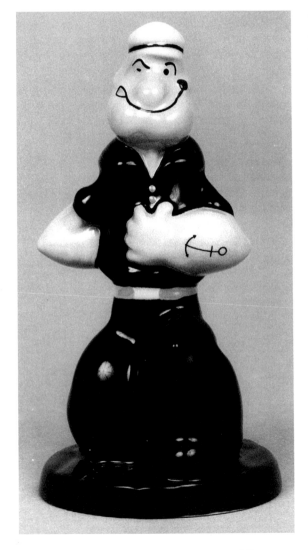

Popeye® *Produced exclusively for David Trower Enterprises in a limited edition of 2000. The 41/2 inch high model retails at £35/$70 and is the first in a set which will comprise: Olive Oil, Brutus and Pluto*

Post War Revitalisation

The immediate post war period for those trying to restart their businesses was in many ways still one of frustration with restrictions and rationing extended into the 1950s. In terms of pottery production white or monochrome wares were still very much the order of the day until about 1952. Fancy and decorative wares were being made but not for sale in the home market, being exclusively for sale only to foreign markets. One of the biggest problems the government had in the late 1940s was to get a healthy balance of payments. The war had cost a lot of money, there was a great deal of rebuilding to do and employment to find for all the de-mobbed soldiers, at the same time Britain was in dire need of filling its coffers. One of the best ways of bringing in revenue was to sell as much as industry could to foreign markets, whilst at the same time reducing our own expenditure, one of the reasons why rationing on various so-called luxury items lasted into the 1950s. One of the ways the government induced the development of businesses and industry was to give generous grants and concessions for opening new factories, especially in sites of high unemployment. With the boom in the building industry came a huge increase in demand for electrical wares which were largely supplied by George Wade & Sons, being by that time the biggest manufacturer, with George now Chairman of the *British Electrical Ceramic Manufacturer's Association*.

With the Manchester Pottery working to capacity to produce electrical wares, Wades needed another site to cope with the demand, which is how the Wade (Ulster) connection started. After looking all over the country a suitable site was found in an old linen mill in Watson Street, Portadown, Northern Ireland, which was soon set up for the production of die-pressed electrical porcelain. By 1950 the pottery having had such success became a private limited company. Early on in the 1950s, with falling demand for its electrical products, the pottery diversified, converting its workshops for the production of commemorative and gift wares, using a distinctive blue/grey glaze that become an instantly recognisable characteristic of Wade (Ulster) wares. Despite an almost devastating fire in 1956 Wade (Ulster) carried on, becoming involved with the production of Whimsies as well as developing their own giftware ranges, some of which were designed by William Harper, the head designer for George Wade & Son Ltd. In November 1966, the pottery changed its name to Wade (Ireland) Ltd., its fortunes still finely in the balance.

As with many other potteries during the post-war period it was realised that in order to be competitive and indeed better than your competitors, the wares you produced had to reflect the era in which they were being made, as well as being of good quality. One way of achieving fashionable products was to employ or commission designers and this is what Col. George Wade having gained promotion during the war, set about doing in 1950 when he established an experimental studio. The aim of this studio was to create prototypes or one-off pieces of artistic work exploring the boundaries of pottery production, the works reflecting contemporary artistic styles. To carry out this task Col Wade persuaded a former student of the Burslem School of Art and recent graduate of the Royal College of Art, Colin Melbourne, still in his early 20s to join the company. Much of the work during the brief life of this experimental studio never saw the light of day with the exception of a figurative model by the name of 'Ivy', later known as 'Festival 51'. This figure was unveiled at an exhibition of ceramic wares put on by numerous potteries at the King's Hall, Stoke-on-Trent, venue of regular trade exhibitions. A little known fact is that there was originally meant to be a companion figure to 'Ivy' which was smashed during the setting up of the exhibition.

A range of wares that perhaps might have developed from the work in this studio, although they appeared sometime later, are the curvilinear 'Shooting Star' pieces, promoted as 'beautifully flowing contemporary shapes'.

As we have just seen, there was the definite attempt to 'move with the times', if on a somewhat small scale, during the 1950s with the employment of Colin Melbourne, a highly promising young designer and contemporary of Terrance Conran. As a consequence of his influence the 'Harmony' tableware range was developed with four different surface pattern designs, of which 'Shooting Star' was the most notable, certainly the most 'contemporary', designed to 'fit happily into modern ideas of interior decoration', as promoted in the advertising. Some of the other patterns were 'Fern', 'Parasol' and 'Carnival'. The same new shapes where also being marketed in various two-tone coloured glazes, in line with other potteries such as Poole. Much in the same vein was the 1957 'Zamba' range, the stylish Henry Moore influenced gaping mouthed shapes decorated with dancing native African figures and later decorated with dancing ballerinas. Similar broader shapes were used for the later Walt Disney based 'Fantasia' design in the early 1960s.

During the same period Wade produced some fashionable tablewares with a new shape design called 'Mode', to be replaced later by the 'Flair' range, which featured for the first time the then popular 'snack' or 'TV Tray', which combined a plate and a cup. This new line came in a variety of new pattern designs, from broad bands of colour forming a trellis pattern over the whole surface, to fishes, leaping deer and spiralling ribbons against a festive starburst ground, each hand-painted. Other designs such as 'Plantain' seems to owe a great deal to Denby pottery designs of the period.

In the late 1950s and early 1960s the latest technical innovation, silk-screen printing, was used to produced patterns for the 'Mode' range, as well as the new shape, 'Flair', introduced in about 1956. The new patterns, 'Sunflower', 'Fern', 'Galaxy', 'Red Polka' and 'Carnival', were very distinctive with solid lines and blocks of bright colours. Some patterns, such as 'Carnival' and 'Fern' appeared on later versions of the 'Harmony' range. Later in the 1960s the patterns reverted to a more popularist approach reflected in the pattern names, 'Violets', 'Summer Rose' and 'Wood Mist' amongst others. Most of these new patterns were designed either by Georgina Lawton or Robert Barlow, who together with the modeller Frank Garbutt, formed the resident design team of the period, Robert Barlow as chief designer.

Many potteries during this period made use of the services of outside or free-lance designers, a relatively new and growing form of employment for recent graduates from the Royal College of Art and other such design schools. Wade were no exception, employing Michael Caddy to design a range of coffee sets and storage jars for Ducor, with its own backstamp, in the 1960s. The designs where quite abstract, 'Siamese' being one pattern name, being produced in two or three colourways using dark colours, blue, black and green, combined with silver or gold. The 'Riviera' patterned storage jars had six different designs produced on three coloured grounds, all with gold finials. Michael Caddy also designed the very contemporary 'Topline' range in 1963 that consisted of a series of vases, dishes and storage jars, with six silk-screen printed and moulded low-relief designs. The latter reflected in the equally contemporary mono-chrome glazed sculptural 'Flaxman' bud vases. Other free-lance designers' work can be seen in the highly stylised 'Gems' tile inset designs of Rhys and Jean Powell, along with other figurative tile designs.

With all the interest in the Wade Whimsies, Disney characters, etc, during the 1950s and 1960s, it seems to me that, in terms of collecting, there is a large gap in market for all the 'stylish' wares made for the 'contemporary' home.

The 1950s and 1960s designs mentioned above were meant to have a short shelf-life, reflecting the fast changing fashions and fads of the period, in general production being restricted to relatively small quantities. It would certainly appear that it is difficult to find such wares today. With all the current enthusiastic interest being shown by collectors in the 1950s and 1960s period I wonder how long it will be before some of the above pieces become highly sought after.

Wade Whimsies

Shortly after the war Col. George Wade's son, Anthony Wade, who had joined George Wade & Son Ltd in 1947, became joint managing director in 1949. There then followed perhaps the most vital period for the Wade Potteries during which time Tony Wade was to play a pivotal role in the birth of what has since made the name of Wade a household word.

Exactly how Whimsies came into being is still a matter of conjecture, perhaps it should remain so, but whatever the chain of events were and whoever was responsible for the initial idea, what cannot be denied is the sheer simplicity of the concept. That the idea of using an already existing process of manufacture, which had been in daily use making of hundreds of thousands of die-cast industrial porcelain insulators for so many years, should be turned into making mass market gift ware, once a little colour had been added, was so obvious that the suggestion the idea first came from Colonel Wade's daughter, Iris, smacks of the truth. Only someone one step removed from the daily business concerns and almost tunnel vision involvement in the running a group of companies could have come up with such a suggestion. The idea of using the raw materials, processes of manufacture and firing methods to make something other than that for which they were intended was nothing new, although you would have thought that those in charge of the such firms would have wanted to make the most of any methods of business getting they could. The wares made at the Doulton Lambeth studio in London, during the late nineteenth century, are a typical example, the main business which had been going for many years being the manufacture of salt-glazed stoneware drain pipes, water filters, chemical containers and sanitary wares until the production of Art wares was suggested by the neighbouring Lambeth School of Art. Another pottery to go down this road and one that had been making porcelain insulators since the very beginnings of electricity in the 1860s, long before Wade's started to make such wares, was Bullers. In 1934 a studio was established at Bullers thanks to the efforts of one of the most important ceramic designers and teachers in the Potteries this century, Gordon M. Forsyth. It was he who persuaded Bullers to sell him some of their true hard porcelain body, then to fire his student's pieces. Later, following the arrival of Anne Potts, Bullers were persuaded to set up and fund an internal studio. By 1935 some 66 pieces of the new studio's wares were chosen to be exhibited at the Exhibition of British Art in Industry held in Burlington House.

Wade's had produced a number of comic animal models (similar to those of Sylvac) and figures before the war using the slip-cast technique. It was the whimsical character of these figures whose production was revived in the late 1940s, that probably gave the name to the next generation of figures – Whimsies.

Following the first prototype of a horse it was decided to market the tiny porcelain animals in a special boxed set of five models. Initially reaction from wholesalers and retailers was not very encouraging, not one order coming from the sample sets. Anthony Wade was not about to give up, deciding to show them at the 1953 British Industries Fair. That proved to be a successful venue after which Whimsies became a major success story. More by chance than design Wade's had hit upon a totally new untapped market, the children of the middle classes along with those with enough pocket money or generous parents, aunts, uncles and grandparents to add to the young collectors new passion. Once part of a set had been established it seemed almost imperative to complete the set. And I speak from experience, presently surrounded by such sets, some boxed, collected in the 1960s.

The first boxed set of Whimsies, that had such an impact at the trade fair, included a horse in the centre surrounded by a poodle, a spaniel, a stag and a squirrel. Anthony Wade seeing the possibilities of these miniature models then employed a designer and modeller, William K. Harper, specifically for the task of coming up with new Whimsey models. It was largely due to the efforts of William Harper, better known as Bill Harper, that the success of the Wade Whimsies was assured. Bill was employed from 1954 to 1962, becoming Head Designer and a junior director, designing not only all the early Whimsey animals but also the T.T. tray, silhouette series, the seagull boat, various posy bowls, the Irish song figures, Irish teapots and many other items too numerous to mention.

The making of Whimsies was not as straightforward as might at first appear, as with most processes of manufacture, and Whimsies had their own unique limitations and restrictions, as well as some benefits, as Bill Harper was to point out in 1959 during a series of correspondence in the ceramics trade press and a local newspaper, the *Evening Sentinel*. From this correspondence we can perhaps understand some of the criteria which, as a designer/modeller, Bill was working under. In a reply to his article in the *Pottery & Glass Record* (March 1959), Bill details some of the conditions which a designer working in a mass-production factory was under. He states that "There must be five figures in the set (one centrepiece and four others). They must be in some sort of proportional relationship to each other. Each figure must fit inside a space 2 inch. by 2 inch by 1 inch or less. At least three of the figures must be delivered from two-part moulds, the others from three-part moulds. The seam must not run over the face because the fettlers might cut it about. There must be no easily broken parts. Colours are all underglaze on high-fired porcelain, which means a limited palette of pale browns and greys, with a deep blue and some few glazes." He then goes on to explain that spots and stripes cannot be used for technical reasons (the colours would bleed leading to fuzzy edges) and amongst other things the boxes had to sell for a price of 3 shillings and 11 pence (1959 prices). After having contended with all this the designer must still bring the figures to life through asserting his own personal identity and not a little ingenuity. One of the concessions of the material, however, was that by using a high-fired porcelain body the figures could have a high degree of fine detail which, thanks to the use of metal die-casting, could be reproduced up to 100,000 times before any loss of detail.

Apart from the above considerations the designer must be aware of and take into account the process of manufacture and in this case these processes were unlike any other being used in the Potteries. The closest process was that being used in the tile industry and perhaps the manufacture of buttons, items being made by pressing clay dust in metal moulds or dies. Whimsey figures were formed in steel dies which had been made up from a master figure, the detail in the steel being engraved by hand. A wet-pressed porcelain dust was then compressed in the steel dies under considerable pressure, forming the final model in only a few seconds. Something like 30,000 such models could be made using this process in day. Once the models had dried the rough edges of the mould line would be fettled or taken off, so that the model could then be painted before being coated in the distinctive translucent glaze, applied by a glaze spraying machine. The models were then sent through a tunnel kiln and fired to a temperature of about 1,250 degrees. Having just a single firing had the effect of making the colours appear to be warm and bright, as well being highly cost effective, doing away with the costs of the bisque firing.

The 1950s was in many respects the Golden era for Wade, brought about by the high profile success of the Whimsies. An important factor in this success was the advertising campaign together with the choice of subjects. Wade's were one of the first potteries to make use of television advertising, with 'an intensive TV campaign featuring the "Whimsies" series (which) will take place during the first two weeks of June'. As reported in the monthly *Pottery Gazette and Glass Trades Review* for 1957. The Whimsies appeared first on a programme called 'What's New' followed by nine further appearances on each week. To accompany the adverts a special jingle was written and further adverts appeared in the *TV Times*. The set being referred to is of course the TV Pet series, based on a popular children's programme. This set was described in trade journals as being 'designed by "Tim"'.

The name and fame of Wade spread far and wide into homes all over the country, largely thanks to the Coronation of 1953 which was responsible for a massive surge in the sale of televisions, leaping to a figure over three million. Wade's had already responded to the rapid growth in demand for televisions making a 'Mode' TV tray in 1953. Not everyone, however, was willing to join in the praise of these playful miniature porcelain figures. Criticism came from the illustrious heights of the Royal College of Art in the form of a thinly veiled attack in an article by Lord Queensberry, concerning the term 'contemporary', one of the burning issues of the day, in which he suggested that the quality of such wares was at best 'mediocre' and if anything 'flamboyant and lacking in style'. Bill Harper felt so incensed by these remarks he wrote a letter to the local paper which was then reprinted and added to, at length, in the pottery trade press, defending Whimsies and public taste.

Of equal importance to the process of manufacture and high profile advertising campaign was the choice of subject matter. Here a collaboration, indeed a friendship, between Tony Wade and Walt Disney ensured a mutually successful partnership that made Wade the envy of many. Along with the success of the various Wade Disney figures, they also marketed various British T.V. characters with figures from Noddy and nursery rhyme figures.

One cannot leave this section on Wade Whimsies without mentioning the adverts which regularly appear in the various trade journals without fail every month, especially from the 1950s onwards, as well as numerous other weekly women's magazines, television times, etc. Looking through the advertising pages of the trade journals at the various adverts it certainly couldn't be said that Wade were amongst the pioneers but they certainly had a style that was all their own. It is also interesting to note how many other manufacturers were soon to start making and advertising their own versions of miniature animal sets, most notably J. H. Weatherby & Sons Ltd., with 'Alice in Wonderland', 'Zookies' and 'Sea Twinks', amongst others, as well as boxed sets such as 'Billy Smart's Circus Set' produced by the Keele Street Pottery and individual animals by the Studio Szeiler pottery. The ltater seemingly having a connection with Wades', certainly some of their models bear a striking resemblance to Wade models, if somewhat larger, such as their version of the Tortoise, Wades' biggest selling model, as well as other pieces such as a model of a duck which is to all intents exactly the same.

Noddy & Big Ears from the Noddy Collection, produced exclusively for UK International Ceramics Ltd in a limited edition of 1500. Retail price for the pair, £68.00/$135

32

*Typical **J. & W. Wade & Co.** decorative **Flaxman Tile Works** stylised tiles showing Persian influenced colour and decoration as well as Art Nouveau stylised patterns. Other tiles produced for fireplace surrounds had mottling of differing strengths, some with textured 'Eggshell' or matt effects. Taken from the* Pottery & Glass Record, March 1924. *The Art Nouveau tiles have a value of between £40-£80/$80-$175 each and the Persian-style tiles £30-£70/$50-$150 each.*

*Example of later Wade tiles dating from the 1950s: Each with a **Wee Willie Winkie nursery rhyme** lithographic printed scene. 'Are the children in their Beds? It's past Eight o'clock!'. Marked – Wade. England. 3 inches square. (£20-£40/$40-$80).*

*'**Wee Willie Winkie Runs through the town**', lithographic printed scene. (£20-£40/$40-$80). The same designs were also used on oval wall plaques. (£300-£400/$550-$800)*

*A 1930s **Wade tile** in the form of a clock face, the centre pierced, hand painted with a Roman numeral dial, a bird in flight above a basket of flowers below in the centre. Marked B.C.M. Wades. England. 6 inches square. These are very rare therefore the value will be between £40-£60/$80-$125.*

1960s tile designs. Designed by Rhys and Jean Powell on H. & R. Johnson blanks and sold through 'Cristal' brand name. (£20-£30/$40-$60)

*Large and small **Alsatian**, designed by Jessie Van Hallen, 10¼ins high and 4¾ ins high respectively. The former with a value of £140-£160/$275-$325 and the latter £50-£200/$100-$400.*

A group of figures by Jessie Van Hallen. *Front:* **Strawberry Girl**, **Tessa**, **Anton**, **Alice**. *Middle:* **Carnival**, **Elf 2**, **Humoresque**. *Top:* **Pompadour**, **Bride**, **Curtsey**. *To find any of these figures on their original lamp bases is very unusual and will certainly add to the value. One point worth noting is that only a maximum of 40 watts should be used in these figurative lamps, preferably less, so that the cellulose coating can be maintained. The values are much as before except for the figure of Anton, which if in good condition can be worth between £100-£200/$200-$400.*

A group of 'Scintillite' coated figures by Jessie Van Hallen, including; 'Daisette', 'Christina', 'Carmen', 'Helga', 'Argentina' and 'Gloria' in the centre. The tallest figure in this group is 'Christina' at about 11ins high.

*A group of figures by Jessie Van Hallen. Front: **Zena**, two small figures of **Jose**, **Rhythm**. Top: **Cherry**, **Pavlova**, **Cherry**, unknown. Values – £150-£350/$300-$700 for larger figures and £80-£100/$160-$200 for Jose. Again notice the colour variations of the duplicates. (See listings for details)*

A group of figures by Jessie Van Hallen. Front: **Zena**, *two* **Sunshine** *figures and two* **Curtsey** *figures. Top: unknown,* **Grace**, **Mimi** *and two figures of* **Springtime**. *Values of these vary considerably according to condition. In perfect condition the dancing and larger figures can be worth between £150-£350/$300-$700, according to size, but flaked, damaged or restored as little as £30-£60/$60-$120. One of the most obvious features of these figures is the relative freedom of colours that could be used. This is particularly noticeable on the duplicate figures. It is also worth noting that the figure of Springtime is very similar to a figure called Greta, the former having a larger rocky base compared to the smaller and smoother base of Greta. Some of these late 1920s Jessie Van Hallen figures were later made using underglaze colours and fired. The value of these is usually higher than their respective cellulose figure. (See listings for details)*

A group of figures by Jessie Van Hallen. *Front:* **Barbara**, **Jeanette**, *two figures of* **Snow White**, **Jeanette**. *Middle: two figures of* **Romance**. *Top:* **Sadie** *and* **Lotus**. *The values for most of these figures will be as before, according to their condition. (See listings for details)*

Snow White and The Seven Dwarfs (Disney Characters copyright The Walt Disney Company) 1938. Designed by Jessie Van Hallen. Snow White 6¼ ins high and the dwarfs from 3½ ins to 4 ins high. In perfect condition a complete set of these figures can be worth between £1000-£2500/$2000-$5000 depending on the condition.

Sonia. A cellulose wall mask designed by Jessie Van Hallen. (£300-£500/$600-$1000)

Tony and **Cynthia**. Modelled by Jessie Van Hallen on the children of George Wade. In this condition they are worth between £100-£150/$200-$300 each.

40

*A collection of **animal figurines** dating from the 1930s and 1940s. These are very similar, sometimes identical to animals made by other potteries such as Shaw & Copestake, Sylvac Works and the Price Bros. of Burslem. In the late 1940s and 1950s Wadeheath used up surplus stock of the smaller animals by placing them on bases with miniature flower vases. The largest animals are worth between £60-£150/$120-$300 and the small posy vases £10-£15/$20-$30.*

***The Thistle and Rose Chess Set.** Designed by Ann Whittet and modelled by Frederick Mellor in 1980, the pieces are based on historical figures of the royal houses dating from the 16th century. In perfect condition and complete with the box the value will be between £600-£800/$1200-$1600, without the box between £400-£600/$800-$1200.*

41

*A collection of **moulded jugs** dating from the 1930s and 1940s. Including a **'Lambeth Walk'** pitcher (top right), circa 1939, many of which were produced as musical versions. £200-£350/$400-$700.*

*A collection of **Royal Commemorative wares** related to the coronation of Queen Elizabeth II, 2nd June, 1953. With values ranging from £20-£30/$40-$60 for the mug in the front row to £100-£120/$200-$250 for the two handled vase.*

A moulded biscuit box and cover and a cheese dish and cover with bird finials. Late 1930s. £40-£60/$80-$120 each. **Pig family cruet set** *and a* **Rabbit family cruet set***, 1940's, both formerly individual figures. £150-£250/$300-$500.*

A very rare sample of the **Snow White tableware set** *produced in 1938 to coincide with the new animated Walt Disney movie. (£300-£500/$600-$1000)*

*A part **Snow White and the Seven Dwarfs children's tea set** dating from about 1938. Yet another product relating to the new Walt Disney picture, Wade Heath & Co. having been granted the sole production rights for using Walt Disney characters on their products in 1934. (A complete boxed set will be worth between £600-£800/$1200-$1600).*

*A collection of **Walt Disney character children's teapots and cups**. The teapots are about 3½ inches high and each will be worth between £200-£300/$400-$600.*

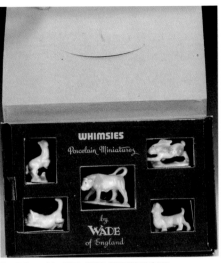

Set 1. The first of the boxed sets sold in 1953. £50-£80/$100-$160.

Set 2. Issued in 1954. £120-£200/$240-$400.

Whimsies

Between 1953 and 1959 ten sets of Whimsies were produced. initially they were sold just as a complete boxed set, only later were they sold individually in their own boxes to make them more affordable. The majority of the sets were designed by William Harper, the odd numbers of which were made in Burslem and the even numbers being made in Ireland. The first sets were all made in limited numbers, the first five of the ten being made in far fewer numbers than the last five sets. Following the success of certain miniature animals in the late 1960s, a new range was produced, the first set being issued in 1971 the twelfth and last set being released in 1984. Each of the sets had different coloured boxes.

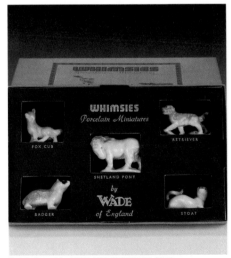

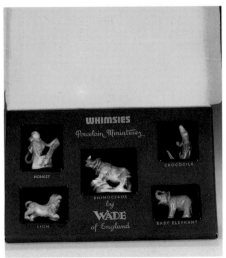

Set 3. Issued in 1955. £80-£120/$160-$240.

Set 4. Issued in 1955. £80-£120/$160-$240.

Set 5. Issued in 1956. £70-£100/$140-$200

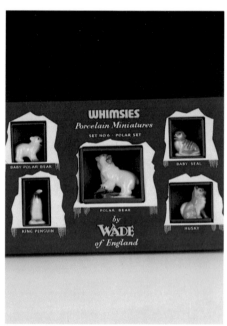

Set 6. Issued in 1956. £60-£90/$120-$175.

Set 7. Issued in 1957. £80-£120/$160-$240.

Set 8. Issued in 1958. £60-£90/$120-$180.

Set 9. Issued in 1958. £80-£100/$160-$200.

Set 10. Issued 1959. £220-£300/$440-$600.

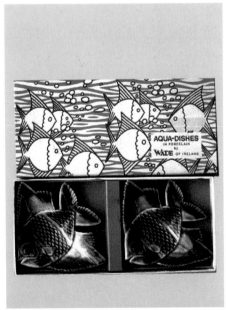

Boxed set of 'Flying Birds' made in Ireland 1956-59. £30-£50/$60-$100.

Boxed set of 'Aqua-Dishes' 1958-60. Set 1 Angel Fish (Wade Ulster). These were made both in England and Ireland (£10-£20/$20-$40.

Nursery Rhyme Figures. *From left to right – **Blyken**, **Wyken**, **Nod**. This shows both types of figure with the 1948-52 models with flowers on the base in the front and the 1952-58 version without the flowers. (£120-£150/$2400-$300 each) These models with the flowers are £10-£20/$20-$40 more expensive.*

Nursery Rhyme Figures. *From left to right – **Poorman**, **Tinker**, **Tailor** and the two versions of **I've a Bear Behind**. £120-£180/$240-$350 each*

48

*Bottom left: **The Whimsies British Character set**, 1959, of the **Pearly King and Queen** (£90-£120/$175-$250), a **Fishmonger** and a **Lawyer** (£120-£150/$230-$300). Three of the five comical novelty animal sets (£10-£15/$20-$30 each), dating from 1955-60 with the Irish Wade 'Pex' Fairy promotional figure (£200-£300/$400-$600) made for Pex stockings between 1948-50. Later incorporated onto a candle holder. **Kissing Rabbits**, 1930s (£60-£90/$120-$175). Beware of an identical pair, unmarked, not made by Wade. **Standing Rabbits** also from the 1930s (£60-£90/$120-$175). The last two being slip-cast under glazed figures. Middle: The Walt Disney characters from **The Sword and the Stone**, 'Hat Box' Series made between 1956-65 with, **Madam Mim (Hen)**, **Archimedes (Owl)**, **Merlin as Hare**, **The Girl Squirrel**, **Merlin as Caterpillar** and **Merlin as Turtle** (see listings for details). Top: The **Aquarium Set** dating from 1975-80 with the only piece missing being the arched bridge (see listings for details).*

*Bottom: The **Noddy series** was introduced in 1958, taken from the Enid Blyton television characters. Each figure with it's original box will be worth between £30-£100/$60-$200, with the exception of Noddy whose value is £150-£200/$300-$400. Top: **Huckleberry Hound**, **Yogi Bear** and **Mr Jinks**, 1959-60, (£180-£220/$350-$450 the set). Based on the Hanna-Barbera cartoon characters.*

*Front: 'Donald Duck' teapot, small size (£400-£600/$800-$1200). The remainder of the animals are from the 'Disneys' Blow-Up series **Lady and the Tramp** and **Bambi**, dating from 1961-65. The values of these figures varies dramatically with some, **Dachie** for example being very rare. **Thumper** (£160-£180/$320-$350), **Bambi** (£70-£90/$140-$175), **Si** (£100-£120/$200-$240), **Am** (£100-£120/$200-$240), **Jock** (£300-£350/$600-$700), **Dachie** (£300-£350/$600-$700), **Trusty**, £120-£140/$240-$275). Top: **Tramp** (£190-£210/$375-$420), **Scamp** (£100-£120/$200-$240), **Lady** (£120-£150/$240-$300), **Fawn** money bank dating from 1987 (£20-£30/$40-$60).*

'Bell's Whisky Decanter' commemorating the marriage of HRH Prince Charles and Lady Diana Spencer, 1981 (£700-£900/$1400-$1800). **Bisto Kids**, Boy and Girl salt and pepper shaker, mid 1970s, (£60-£90/$120-$180). **Beneagles Scotch Whisky decanter** modelled in the form of a bear, produced between 1981-87 (£70-£100/$140-$200). **Toby Jim** Jug (£50-£80/$100-$160). **Sandeman** decanter, produced between 1958-61 (£80-£100/$160-$200). **Scottie** teapot, 1953-55, designed by George Lawton, produced with four different tartan decorated lids (£180-£220/$360-$440). **Carrington's Beers** toby jug (£80-£120/$160-$240). Prices are for full decanters and/or complete boxes.

Duck posy bowl (£25-£35/$50-$70). **Ruddy Duck** *is an unmarked hollow model made in the 1970s in a limited edition of 3400 (£150-£200/$300-$400).* **Wren** *is one of the Connoisseur's Collection, dating from the early 1980s (£200-£300/$400-$600).* **Cockatoo spirit container** *made in 1961 for Henry Stratton & Co distillers (£100-£150/$200-$300).* **Swan Egg-cup,** *mid 1950s (£15-£25/$30-$50).*

A collection of 1950s **Teenage Pottery** *heart-shaped trinket boxes and plaques, produced in the early 1960s – Tommy Steele, Cliff Richard, Marty Wilde and Frankie Vaughan, with a Marty Wilde plaque (between £50-£200/$100-$400 each).*

*The **World of Survival** series, 1978-82. These animals were manufactured under licence to Survival Anglia Limited after their award winning television series. There were two sets with six animals in each. Due to the high costs involved there were very limited numbers made (£1200-£1600/$2400-$3200 first set; £1800-£2300/$3600-$4600 second set).*

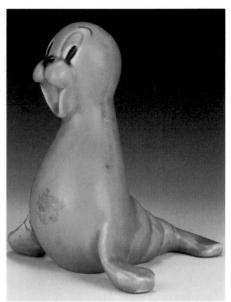

'Salty' The Seal. Marked: Wadeheath England. By Permission Walt Disney. 6¹/₂ins high. This dates from the late 1930s and is highly sought after with a value of between £200-£250/$400-$500.

The current auction World Record Holder for a single piece of Wade at £1700/$3400. Underglazed model of **Ermine on a Rock** modelled by Faust Lang, dated 1939, 9¹/₂ inches high. (Courtesy of the Potteries Antiques Centre Ltd)

An underglazed model of a **Seated Panda**, dated 1939, probably a Faust Lang model (with a value between £800-£1200/$1600-$3200, one having recently sold for £970/$1940 (hammer)).(Courtesy of the Potteries Antiques Centre Ltd)

*A group of hard paste porcelain animals modelled by 'The famous Faust Lang of Oberammergau . . .' as the advertising by Wade announced, as well as later animal models by Bill Harper. Front: **Baby Polar Bear 'Blow-up'**, 4³/₄ inches high (£180-£220/$350-$450), **Baby Seal 'Blow-up'** (£200-£250/$400-$500) with **Polar Bear 'Blow-up'** (£180-£220/$350-$450) above, standing 6 inches high, all three modelled by Bill Harper dating from 1962.*
*Top: **Stag**, 8³/₄ inches high (£700-£900/$1350-$1800), **Polar Bear**, 7³/₄ inches high (£1200-£1500/$2500-$3000) and **Panther** 8¹/₂ inches high (£800-£1000/$1500-$2000) all modelled by Faust Lang in the mid 1930s. In terms of value, Faust Lang models are some of the most sought after and expensive pieces of Wade, each with a value in the region of £800-£1800/$1500-$3500.*

A Faust Lang *model of* **Budgerigar**, *8 inches high (£200-£300/$400-$600) and a Faust Lang model of a* **Woodpecker**, *6 inches high (£200-£300/$400-$600). These models of birds do not seem to have the popularity of the more expressive animals and therefore do not command such high prices. (Courtesy of the Potteries Antiques Centre Ltd)*

Mr & Mrs Rabbit, *produced in the late 1940s, 3¹/₂ ins high, £80-£120/$160-$240. Two* **Angelic figures**, *part of three different sets produced from 1959 to through the 1960s. These figures can be found standing, sitting or kneeling and were later added to the bases of candleholders, trays and the like. (£20-£30/$40-$60).*

*A rare Wadeheath Walt Disney model of **Mickey Mouse**, circa 1934 recently sold for £1400/$2800. (Courtesy of the Potteries Antiques Centre Ltd)*

*Three miscellaneous models of **Kittens playing**, late 1930s (£50-£60/$100-$120). **Jerry** of 'Tom and Jerry' (Metro-Goldwyn-Mayer Inc. Copyright), a little under 2 inches high (£30-£40/$60-$80) and a model of a **seated smiling Rabbit**, 1940s, (£40-£60/$80-$120).*

*Two animals from a large collection of over 30 'Disney' characters, 1981-87, with **Rolly** and **Lucky** (£50-£70/$100-$140) on the left and **Am** and **Si** (£90-£100/$0180-$200) on the right. With the current renewed interest in the latest version of 101 Dalmatians the former will undoubtedly rise in value. Lastly **Tom** (£30-£40/$60-$80), partner to Jerry above.*

Alphabet Train, *produced between 1958-59. The limited production of this set makes it quite sought after and if it's in good condition and boxed the value can be between £400-£600/$800-$1200.*

*A **collection of Minikins** figurines, produced between 1956-59 and issued in three series (£10-£30/$20-$60).*

*A set of ten **T.V. Pets**, produced between 1959-65, with nine dogs and a cat each with a value of £30-£50/$60-$100 with their boxes or £20-£40/$40-$80 without.*

Lucky Leprechauns made by Wade (Ireland) Ltd between 1956-86. The tallest figure (2¹/₄ inches high) is 'Lucky Leprechaun' (£15-£25/$30-$50) surrounded by 'Little People' (£10-£15/$20-$30) carrying out their various trades.

The Seven Dwarfs (miniature) from Snow White and the Seven Dwarfs, 1980s, unrecorded ?????? Ask owner – £800-£1200/$0000-$0000.

A rare model of **Pogo**, *based on the newspaper cartoon strip, produced in 1959 and modelled by* William Harper *(£250-£450/$500-$900). A slip-cast and unmarked model of a* **Cartoon Boy** *again by* William Harper, *1950s, (£250-£450/$500-$900).* **Mr Penguin** *pepper shaker (£120-£150/$240-$300) and* **Benny** *(£80-£120/$160-$240) from the Penguin Family produced in the late 1940s. Mr Penguin can also be found in the same colouring as Benny.*

Dilly *and* **Mrs Duck** *from the* **Quack Quack Family**, *(1952-60) designed by* Robert Barlow *(£80-£100/$160-$200 each).* **Drake** *usually marked Wade England in ink (£50-£80/$100-$160) and* **Seagull**, *1 inch high, made by Wadeheath in the 1940s (£100-£150/$200-$300).*

Robin Hood and *Maid Marion* from the *Sherwood Forest* Series, 1989-90, made in a limited edition of 5000 for Posner Associates of Canada (£20-£30/$40-$60). *Poorman* from the *Nursery Rhyme Figurine* Series, c1950-55, designed by Nancy Great-Rex (£100-£150/$200-$300). *The last figure looks very like the model* **Doleful Dan** *from the animal series produced during the late 1930s through to the 1960s but is in fact a* **Studio Szeiler copy** *and a very accurate one, made by Joseph Szeiler who set up in business on his own in the 1950s, having been a caster for Wadeheath.*

A set of Wade Ceramics Ltd **Dinosaurs**, 1993, designed by Barbara Cooksey *and modelled by* Ken Holmes *(£10-£20/$20-$40 for the set).*

*A collection of money boxes – **Peter the Polar Bear**, 1988 (£10-£20/$20-$40), **Bambi** (£30-£50/$60-$100). The **Natwest Seated Panda**, 1989, (£30-£40/$60-$80) and the **Thorntons Chocolate Wagon** (£20-£30/$40-$60).*

*A set of **Westminster Piggy Banks**, introduced in 1983, (£100-£150/$200-$300).*

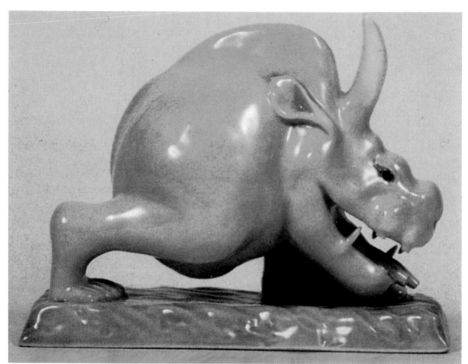

*A rare unrecorded underglazed model of **Running Spoof**, hand-written mark A G Fiddes Watt, England in blue (£250-£350/$500-$700). (Courtesy of the Potteries Antique Centre Ltd.)*

***Pluto** and one of the **Quinpuplets** dating again from the late 1930s and again rare so the value will be between £300-£400/$600-$800 each.*

Old Nanny an early underglazed seated figure, 1935-39, probably designed by Jessie Van Hallen, 9 inches high (£400-£500/$800-$1000).

Hille Bobbe by Jessie Van Hallen. 10ins high. (£200-£400/$400-$800).

The **Candlestick Maker** (£300-£350/$600-$700) and the **Butcher** (£175-£200/$350-$400) from the **Nursery Rhyme** series, 1950s, designed by Nancy Great-Rex.

Snow White and the Seven Dwarfs, 1981-86, slip cast figures (£600-£900/$1200-$1800).

*An unusual model of a **Seated Deer**, possibly a prototype (£100-£150/$200-$300). The **Big Bad Wolf** musical jug, 1935 (£300-£400/$600-$800).*

*Part of a set of **Irish Character Figures**, 1970s to 1986, each with an ink stamp – Made in Ireland. (£15-£30/$30-$60 each).*

*Part of a set of **Nursery Favourites**, 1972-81, each one worth between £15-£20/$20-$40.*

*A set of four **Guinness promotional figurines**, 1968. These had a limited issue making the figures quite sought after (£60-£100/$120-$200 each on average).*

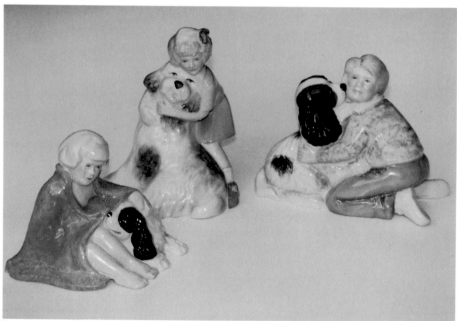

*Three figurative groups from the **Welcome Home** series, introduced in 1993, modelled by Ken Holmes, produced in a limited edition of 2500 numbered items (£25-£35/$50-$70).*

*A set of four hand-decorated **Sophisticated Ladies**, although marked My Fair Ladies, 1991-92, by Wade Ceramics Ltd. These did not prove popular, being withdrawn quite quickly (£70-£80/$140-$160 on average).*

*Figure from the two sets of **My Fair Ladies**, 1990-92, showing some of the various colourways used for these figures (£20-£40/$40-$80 each).*

69

*A Wade advertisement for a set of colour lithographs of **Emett cartoons**, Taken from the* Pottery Gazette, May 1958.

*A Wade advertisement for the **Zamba** series of wares, 1957. With vases and dishes in the sculptured New Style of the period. Taken from the* Pottery Gazette, *June 1957.*

*Three graduated **McCallum** water jugs. These jugs were produced in mulitcoloured versions and in monochrome. The tallest 6³/₄ inches high (£50-£80/$100-$160) and the smallest 2³/₄ inches high (£30-£50/$60-$100).*

Roll out the Barrel tankard 'Soldier', introduced in 1940 (£40-£60/$80-$120) and 'Winston Churchill' (£40-£60/$80-$120).

Pet-face dish, produced between 1959-60, in the shape of a **Siamese Cat** (£20-£30/$40-$60) and a **Pekinese Dog** (£20-£30/$40-$60), both made to be used as a wall hung ornament. **Man in a Boat**, 1978-84, a variation on the boat with a seagull (1961), (£30-£50/$60-$100) and **Redskin** dish (£15-£20/$30-$40).

A set of three graduated **Yacht Wall Plaques**, 1955, made by Wade (Ireland), the largest 4½ inches high (£40-£70/$80-$140 each).

Cherub Bowl, produced between 1957-59 (£15-£20/$30-$40).

Prototype decanter made for Wade (PDM) Ltd by Wade, Heath & Co Ltd (£40-£70/$80-$140).

Beefeater bottle pourer, one of a series of pourers, this one marked for Wade Regicor (£20-£40/$40-$80).

A wall face mask of Frolic, circa 1930 (£250-£350/$500-$700).

*Special commissions made by Wade for G & G Collectables are from left to right and edition size: **Yogi Bear** (1500), **Boo-Boo** (1500), **Scoopy Doo** (2000) and **Scrappy Doo** (2000), all of which except Boo-Boo which will be released in August 1997 are sold out and are fetching a premium over issue price.*

*A hand painted **Flaxman Ware Wadeheath Wall Plaque**, 1930s, 12½ inches diameter, with a very well painted scene of a finch on a branch (£120-£180/$240-$360).*

*Three figures from the **Law and Order** set issued by Elaine and Adrian Crumpton in a limited edition of 2000. **The Burglar** (£30-£40/$60-$80) and **The Policeman** (£25-£35/$50-$70) were issued in 1993, whilst the **Lawyer** (£20-£30/$40-$60) was issued in 1994. **The Prisoner** (1995) completes the set. See pages 89 and 91 for variations.*

*A set of five graduated elephants, **Treasures**, produced in 1956. Like the Alphabet Train the Elephant Chain was only produced in limited numbers therefore the value for the set will be between £200-£300/$400-$600.*

*Slip-cast porcelain models of **Brighton Pavilion**, 1988 (£10-£15/$20-$30 each).*

*Part of a set of **San Francisco Mini Mansions**, known as '**Painted Ladies**', 1984-86, (£30-£50/$60-$100) together with a miniature Cable Car (£50-£80/$100-$160).*

*Three of a series of **Lesney Trays** made between 1968-75, the metal ornaments being made by Lesney Industries Ltd and fixed onto the trays. On the left is a model of an **Open Double Decker Bus**, in the centre a model of the **Sante Fe** and on the right is a model of a **Horse Drawn Bus** (£30-£50/$60-$100 each).*

Dracula from Nexus/Wade to commemorate the 40th anniversary of Hammer Horror Films

Prototype **British Bulldog** made in 1940.

Pegasus Posy Bowl, produced between 1958-59. Although produced in the 1950s the style of this bowl has the sharp angular look of a late 1920s Art Deco piece (£50-£60/$100-$120). Snowman, the second of the Wade special limited editions, sold through the official Wade Collectors Club, issued in December 1994, (£30-£40/$60-$80).

A collection of Gaffer Tetley tableware made for Lyons Tetley, introduced in 1992. The cruet set (£15-£25/$30-$50) and the cookie jar and biscuit box (£30-£50/$60-$100).

*A **collection of Prototypes**, most slip cast. Many of these figurines were designed by* William Harper.

*On the left is a Wade, Heath & Co. Ltd model of **Mrs Duck** (£125-£150/$250-$300) from the Quack Quack nursery ware family made in the 1950s. On the right is a **Studio Szeiler version** made in the 1960s.*

Modern Developments

In 1950 Wade Heath & Co. Ltd became involved with the retailers, Reginald Corfield (Sales) Ltd, whose offices were in the outskirts of London. The venture known as Wade Regicor soon developed the lucrative market of pub and bar advertising for clients in the brewery and distillery trades. By 1969, having virtually cornered the market, with little in the way of competition left, Wade's set up their own company, Wade (PDM) Ltd, which was almost exclusively set up for the promotion, marketing and design of the advertising wares.

Wade's devotion to their workers can be seen in 1959 when the pottery introduced a new security scheme, which was believed to be the first of its type, where by 'in the event of any redundancy, increased periods of notice would be given according to years of service'. A scheme that is now run by a large section of industry and business today.

The period of 1960s to the 1980s was one of fluctuation and takeovers during which time Anthony Wade took the reins of the company after his father, Colonel Wade retired, albeit a semi-retirement, at Christmas 1971. Mergers seemed to be affecting every industry and business. If you were big enough and you wanted to expand you merely bought up your ailing competitor or indeed branched out into other avenues by buying up a business that you could link in sympathetically with your own. Wade Potteries Ltd., as with other major potteries, started to acquire sites in different parts of the country. Having moved into Scotland, taking over three firms during the 1960s and 1970s, it wasn't long before the recession of the late 1970s and early 1980s meant that resources had to be drawn back in. Throughout this period the demand for tiles reduced, A. J. Wade Ltd suffering as a result, until in 1970 operations were finally ceased.

The niche that Wade have made for themselves over the years, indeed made their own, is the large or small scale Premium & Promotion commissions being able to produce just a few thousand items or several million pieces of a single object, dependent on the customers' order. These 'free-gifts' with the purchase of certain products have eagerly been taken up over the years by American and Canadian manufacturers ordering large sets of Wade's miniature porcelain animals, the incentive being to build up your collection.

Today Wade is very much alive and kicking, but there have been some dramatic changes. The biggest change was that in January 1990 Wade Potteries Ltd. was taken over by Beauford plc, who had been acquiring several companies during this period. Wade Potteries Ltd. was no longer an independent company, it's name changing to Wade Ceramics Ltd., now under control of the Beauford group, with Wade (Ireland) Ltd, renamed Seagoe Ceramics Ltd., reporting directly to the new parent company rather than Wade. Tablewares continued to be made at Wade (Ireland)/Seagoe Ceramics Ltd, having only recently re-tooled to make such wares, for a further few years but did not meet with sufficient success and in 1993 the tableware department was closed. The factory was re-tooled again, concentrating this time on industrial and engineering ceramics.

More recently the most significant development under the new ownership has been the building of a new state-of-the-art factory, or should I say manufacturing facility, at Winchester, Kentucky, in the United States of America. Wade Ceramic Fibers, Inc., opened in 1995, making ceramic fibre firelogs for fireplaces and stoves using technology and processes formerly developed by Wade Ceramics UK, employing some sixteen people at the 25,000 square foot premises.

Wade Ceramics Ltd. today are one of the most diversified and successful companies in the Potteries, using some of the most up to date equipment in Europe. They still manufacture a wide range of ceramic products to customer's specifications, such as the now discontinued set of Piggy banks for the National Westminster Bank, a complex multitude of items for the electrical and gas industry, including ceramic coal, log and coke fuel effects for modern fires, looking every bit like the real thing. Ever at the forefront of ceramic design technology they manufacture highly advanced components for use in space, nuclear engineering and the electronics world using high purity alumina.

*From the Flintstones Collection, **Fred and Wilma** along with **Barney and Betty**. Made exclusively for UKI Ceramics Ltd the set is limited to 1500 pieces each and sold in husband and wife pair for £68/£135.*

Prototypes

This is an area that seems to have been largely overlooked in the past with the exception of one case and yet for collectors is perhaps the most lucrative. Prototypes are some of the rarest pieces of Wade on the market, as you might expect. This group is made up of various types of trials to those that were made and painted in different colourways, one colourway being selected the others rejected. Some trials were made up, a colourway chosen but then never put into production. Occasionally there are studies of animals or figures that were out of scale or may have deliberately been made too large as a prototype, the final item being reduced in scale and put into production. There are also those items that, once they were made up, proved to be too difficult to cast properly, some part of the model seemingly always getting stuck or broken during the casting. What you might come across also are pieces with experimental glaze effects, such as matt black, which might appear on solids or cast pieces.

Whatever the reason the fate would have been much the same, stuck on the top shelf in a room along with all the other rejected pieces for a few years, sometimes several years, until they were either thrown out or taken home as mementos by some of the workers who were given or paid for the pieces. In years gone by there was an unwritten rule that workers could have or buy pieces rejected a number of years before as long as they didn't sell them. Moorcroft pottery and Doulton figures being such examples. As with most potteries in Stoke, for that matter anywhere, many such objects often found their way into the homes of the families that owned the pottery, a practice very much alive today. Several years ago when a noted member of the Wade family died many such trials or prototypes came onto the market and have since disappeared into collectors cabinets.

In terms of body there are two distinct types, solid and whole models. The most obvious prototypes are the hollow models, which, as the term implies, have been made by slip-casting and have no base, to speak of. Not being forced into the mould also means that often the features are less detailed, being slightly softer, although this is not always the case as the model was sometimes worked on after casting. The solids where made much as the normal models the clay being forced into moulds. A noticeable feature of such pieces is that they do not usually have a mark either on the side or the base.

As far as the Wade factory is concerned there has recently been a change in attitude towards their recent trials or prototypes, deciding to keep a closer control on such pieces that are now being marked as property of Wade Potteries and are no longer to be allowed off the premises. If anything this will make the market for those that were previously thrown away or sold even keener. Some prototypes are already selling for high hundreds and a few over the £1000/$2000 bracket. The pricing of these old prototypes is very difficult as it basically boils down to whatever the buyer is willing to part with. Simply by implying that there is no price available on these pieces only adds to the myth surrounding these older prototypes.

What is certainly not acceptable is the buying or selling of more recent trails and prototypes. In recent years, having had a change of management, the policy regarding prototypes has changed. It is no longer the practice for any such pieces to leave the factory and for obvious reasons. Trials and prototypes form a very useful library of research that can be dipped into whenever required, either to duplicate a customers' future requirements or to learn from previous designs. With reports of such pieces having left the factory and therefore in circulation, I would suggest that you make sure that any recent models you might like to purchase, if they are limited editions, numbered, etc., have all their documents.

Colour prototype of the first model in the Children of the World series. Issued in a 1000 each of two colourways of Marine Blue and Jade Green. The remainder of the series is pictured on page 21.

Advertising Wares

By far the largest group of wares made by Wade Potteries and the one least recognised by the general public must be their advertising wares. Certainly since the post war period this area has almost been the exclusive domain of the Wade Potteries, initially as a partnership venture under the name 'Wade Regicor' and then running under their own steam as Wade (PDM) Ltd. There can hardly be a public house in Britain or indeed bars on various continents that do not have some Wade ceramics adorning the tables or bar tops. As far as collecting is concerned the wares in this group are not highly sought after by many, although there is a growing core of devoted enthusiasts in countries such as America, Canada and Britain. Within this group the largest number of clients seem to be the breweries and distillers, although others such as Hotel chains, airlines and members of the tobacco industry have placed numerous orders for ashtrays and other promotional items.

The vast majority of advertising related wares have a value under £20-£40/$40-$80 but there are some notable exceptions that have been rapidly increasing in value and are now highly sought after items. The most sought after items in the main are decanters, but of course these would have to have their contents as well as the box to be of greatest value.

Decanters
Bell's Old Scotch Whisky. Since 1988 a special Bell shaped decanter has been produced for United Distillers Bell's whisky every **Christmas** for the UK market and another special design for the South African market. There have also been special issues for royal occasions and commemorating special events. All the decanters have been produced in limited quantities helping to develop the secondary market. In the main the annual UK decanters, produced in green and cream for the first four years then changing to an overall green, are worth between £50-£80, with the exception of 1988 which can be worth between £200-£300/$400-$600. The special decanters for the **South African** market have been produced in the green and cream for the last six years, with designs of '**Curling**', '**Golf**' and '**Fishing**' used between 1992-94 respectively. These appear to be amongst the most collectable , selling for between £250-£300/$500-$600.

Other Bell's decanters such as **Hawaii**, **Wedding** and **Prince Henry** (issued in 1984 to commemorate his birth), boxed and full, are worth between £250-£350/$500-$700, while 'Year of the Sheep' (1991) and 'Year of the Monkey' (1992) are worth between £120-£180/$240-$360. But perhaps the most eagerly sought after of the Bell's decanters, issued in 1981, are the two commemorating **HRH Prince Charles and Lady Diana Spencer**. The full size decanter, issued for £24/$48, is currently selling for between £700-£900/$1400-$1800, while the mini decanter, 4 inches high, that was issued in a limited edition of between 650 to 700 and presented to the workers of the Bell's distillery, seems to selling for £850-£950/$1700-$1950.

Dimple Scotch Whisky commissioned a series of decanters between 1987 to 1990 – Dragon, Year of the Horse, Year of the Snake, each of which are worth between £350-£450/$700-$900. The Dimple Scotch Whiskey – Coat of Arms is worth £150-£200/$300-$400.

Coach decanter made for **Gordon Chaseton** in a limited edition, 6¹/₂ inches high, £180-£280/$360-$560.

Thornton & France Sherry Barrel, 11¹/₄ inches long. Produced in a limited edition of 200 in 1980-81, £120-£180/£240-$360

The **'John Paul Jones'** US Navy and Marine Corps Ships decanter. First commissioned by Prusser's Ltd in 1983, 8³/₄ inches high. £100-£150/$200-$300. The same shape has been subsequently used on various other decanters.

British Airways Liquor Bottle. Modelled in the form of Concorde, 2¹/₄ inches high, £120-£180/$240-£360.

The English Gentleman's Choice decanter, 10 inches high, £100-£150/$200-$300

Sandeman decanter. 8¹/₂ inches high. For George G. Sandeman & Co Ltd. 1958-61, £80-£100/$160-$200.

Baby Chick spirit decanters. 1961. Made for the Guernsey Cream, Advocaat, Channel Islands Fine Distillers Ltd, Guernsey. Sole Concessionaire Rawlings & Son (London) Ltd. A very limited number of these reached the market, sold through Boots the Chemist, following a fire that destroyed the brewery.

Whitbread Pale Ale Train and Tender. Produced between February and March 1979 for Whitbread International Belgium. In all only 140 train decanters and 70 tenders were produced, making them highly sought after, the current value being over £1000/$2000.

Beneagles Scotch Whisky. 4³/₄ inches high. Made by Wade (Ireland) Ltd for Peter Thompson (Perth) Ltd in the form of a brown bear, between 1981-87, £70-£100/$140-$200.

Cockatoo Spirit container. 5 inches high, Commissioned by Henry Stratton & Co in 1961, but seems never to have been used for their original purpose, instead being sold through a UK store. It is generally held that there might have been three graduated Cockatoos and three Penguins all made for Henry Stratton & Co. The largest Cockatoo – £100-£150/$200-$300. The largest Penguin – £50-£70/$100-$140.

Old Parr Tribute decanter. 7 inches high. 1990-91, £300-£400/$600-$800.

Black & White Scotch Whisky decanter, modelled in the form of two Scottie dogs, 7¹/₂ inches high. 1972-1986. £180-£220/$360-$440.

Findlater's Whisky decanters commissioned between 1986-1990, one in the shape of a football and the other as a rugby ball, £80-£120/$160-$240.

The Scotsman whisky decanter, made for **Asprey & Co** in the 1930s, £240-£280/$480-$560.

The Irishman whisky decanter, made for **Asprey & Co** in the 1930s. No price for one of these has been recorded as one has yet to turn up. Unless you know differently??

Irish Mist 9 inches high. 1965-66, £80-£100/$160-$200

The Potteries decanter. This decanter was produced in 1994 and 1995, with some 500 decanters (£150-£200/$300-$400) being given to clients and staff at the Glenngoyne Distillery, Drumgoyne, Scotland, in the first year and 350 in 1995. (£120-£150/$240-$300).

Mugs

Taunton Cider have commissioned numerous mugs since 1974, each in a limited edition of 500, the first 50 being numbered, many decorated with a variety of scenes influenced by eighteenth and nineteenth century designs. The most desirable are the larger two handled mugs that are worth between £40-£70/$80-$140.

Jugs

Charrington's Beer toby jug. 7⅜ inches high. 1960s, £80-£120/$160-$240.

Toby Jim jug. 4⅜ inches high, £50-£70/$100-$140.

The MacCallum water jug. A set of three graduated jugs, the tallest 6¾ inches (£50-£80/$100-$160) and the smallest 2¼ inches (£30-£50/$60-$100). There was also a **MacCallum ashtray**, 4¾ inches diameter (£30-£40/$60-$80).

Money Banks

Lyon's vintage van for Lyon's Tetley		
5¼ inches high	1990	£50-£70/$100-$140
Monster Munch		
6½ inches high	1987-88	£70-£90/$140-$180
Tetley vintage van for Lyon's Tetley		
5¼ inches high	1990	£40-£60/$80-$120
'Brew Gaffer' for Lyon's Tetley		
5¼ inches high	1989-90	£50-£70/$100-$140
J. W. Thornton Ltd delivery van		
4¾ inches high	1993	£40-£50/$80-$100
Rington's Tea delivery van		
5¼ inches high		£50-£70/$100-$140
Boots van		
5¼ inches high		£40-£50/$80-$100

'Sputnik' money box for MacMillan Davies Brunning Ltd on behalf of the Scarborough Building Society.

4¼ inches high	1993	£60-£80/$120-$160
Harrod's Doorman		
6¾ inches high		£50-£60/$100-$120
'Gaffer' for Tetley GB Ltd.		
6 inches high	1996	£40-£60/$80-$120

National Westminster Piggy Bank Family. Produced between 1984-1989 for children under twelve who opened a savings account, each figure being available when six monthly targets had been reached. Once having completed the Piggy Family the account holder was then given a Piggy mug if they joined the National Westminster Bank 100s club. In order of qualification the mugs were:

Woody	5 inches high	£10-£15/$20-$30
Annabel	6³/₈ inches high	£20-£25/$40-$50
Maxwell	6³/₄ inches high	£45-£55/$90-$110
Lady Hillary	7 inches high	£30-£40/$60-$80
Sir Nathaniel	7¹/₄ inches high	£45-£55/$90-$110

Jim Beam van money box. 5¹/₄ inches high. Produced in two different colourways for the 26th Annual Convention, Seattle, Washington, July, 1996, in a limited edition of 305, £60-£80/$120-$160.

Miscellaneous

'Pex' Fairy. Made for Pex Stockings by Wade (Ulster) Ltd. 2³/₈ inches high. 1948-50. This figure is very rare and seems to have been produced in various colourways as well as being incorporated onto a base as a candleholder. The candleholder is generally of higher value, £300-£400/$600-$800.

Guinness Promotional Figures. Made in 1968/9 these figures were produced in a limited number and are therefore very sought after.

Tony Weller	3 inches high	£100-£120/$200-$240
Tweedle Dee & Tweedle Dum	2⁷/₈ inches high	£120-£150/$240-£300
Wellington Boot	3¹/₂ inches high	£100-£120/$200-£240
Mad Hatter	3¹/₄ inches high	£120-£150/$240-$300
Tetley Van Tea Caddy 1994-95	5³/₈ inches high	£70-£90/$140-$180
The Brewmaster, made for Flowers Beer 1960s	5¹/₄ inches high	£180-£220/$360-$440

Robertson's Gollies 'Bandstand' figures. Commissioned in the early 1960s the set contains seven figures, such as the Saxophone player, Trumpet Player, Drummer, etc., each of which are currently worth between £100-£180/$200-$360. These figures, which in this case should have white bases, were reproduced later by another company with black bases. The Wade Golly musician were displayed on a simple white circular bandstand.

Hamm's Bear 'Santa's Helper'. Commissioned by Silver State Specialities in 1995 and 1996 in limited editions, £30-£50/$60-$100.

Whitbread Pin Badge and Ceramic Frog. Only a few thousand of these were made, the frog being attached to the metal badge with double sided tape. The badge – 2¹/₂ inches diameter. The frog – 1¹/₂ inches long. 1987. The value lies in both items being together., £30-£40/$60-$80.

Recent Commissions & Specials

1993

The Burglar – The first piece commissioned by Elaine and Adrian Crumpton in a limited edition of 2000. Later this set was given the name **Law & Order** (£30-£40/$60-$80).

The Policeman – The second of the Law & Order set commissioned by Elaine and Adrian Crumpton. There are two versions of this model, the first with the helmet over the eyes that was issued in a limited edition of 400 (£40-£60/$80-$120) and the second with a painted face issued in an limited edition of 1600 pieces (£25-£35/$50-$70). There would appear to be a number of fakes of the latter model that have a yellow badge and pale blue or black uniform.

Arthur Hare – The first of a series of wares commissioned by C. & S. Collectables run by Russell Schooley and David Chown. This figure was produced in a limited edition of 2000, together with a special presentation box, of which 1650 were produced in a pale blue (£20-£30/$40-$60) and 350 produced in fawn (£40-£60/$80-$120).

Thornton Delivery Van Money Box – Commissioned by J. W. Thornton Ltd. (£40-£50/ $80-$100).

Rex the Retriever – commissioned by Debenhams, in 1993, as a memento for the staff who had been involved in the setting up of a new computerised retrieval system for the financial department. In all 250 Debenham dogs, fixed onto oval mahogany bases, were made and issued to the staff.

1994

Wade Factory Cat Model – Later called 'Burslem' following a competition amongst all the Wade Club members to find the best name for the Wade factory cat. This model was issued free to every new member who joined the Official International Wade Collectors Club in the first year of its existence. Membership cost. (£30-£40/$60-$80)

Special limited edition **Brown Spaniel Dog** (3¼ inches high). Limited edition of 1000 produced for the first U.K. Wade Collectors Fair at the Motorcycle Museum, Birmingham. The whole issue was reported to have sold out within the first three hours of the Fair (£50-£80/$100-$160).

Bear Ambitions Teapots – There were six teapots in this set each designed by Judith Wootton, including: **Admiral Sam, Locomotive Joe, Alex the Aviator, Artistic Edward, Beatrice the Ballerina** and **Musical Marco** (£15-£25/$30-$50).

Bell's Decanter – Christmas 1994 (£40-£60/$80-$120).

Bell's South African Decanter – Christmas 1994 (£220-£280/$440-$560).

London Life Teapots – A set of three teapots each designed by Barbara Cooksey including: **The Guard**, **The Parade** and **The Capital** (£15-£25/$30-$50).

Animal Money Boxes – A set of four monochrome glazed money boxes, including: **Gerty the Jersey** (light brown), **Priscilla the Pig** (pink), **Bob the Frog** (green) and **Lucky the Rabbit** (grey) (£10-£15/$20-$30).

Polcanthus Money Box – Commissioned by Margaret Strickland in a limited edition of 2000, this money box depicted a dinosaur skeleton found on the Isle of Wight (£30-£40/$60-$80).

Lawyer – Commissioned by Elaine and Adrian Crumpton in a limited edition of 2000 pieces. Unlike the former pieces in this set this piece has a transfer printed mark of Wade Made in England, rather than the moulded Wade mark (£20-£30/$40-$60).

Wade Limited Editions – **Fireside Friend**, **Welcome Home**, **Togetherness** – each issued in a limited edition of 2500 and supplied with a hardwood recessed base, these were only available from the Wade factory. The four pieces, Welcome Home having two models, were modelled by Ken Holmes. The third piece in this set, Togetherness, was issued in September 1994 at which time the first two models were still available, indeed in December all four models were still being promoted for their original price £25/$50. Today they are worth £30/£50/$60-$100.

Snowman – First of three Christmas theme figures sold through the Official Wade Collectors Club, in a limited edition of 1500 pieces at £12.50/$25 each (£40-£50/$80-$100).

Tetley Tea Folk Van Caddy – A special promotion by Lyons Tetley in conjunction with Esso Petroleum - launched in September. This had the Gaffer driving the van with his nephew sitting next to him. To obtain one of these you had to collect 200 Tiger Tokens from Esso Service Stations as long as the promotion lasted which was for six months (£70-£90/ $140-$180).

Tales from the Nursery – A set of ten miniatures of traditional nursery rhymes commissioned by Tom Smith Ltd. for their Christmas crackers 1994, including: **Hickory Dickory Dock**, **Bo-Peep**, **Humpty Dumpty**, the **Cat and the Fiddle**, **Doctor Foster**, the **Queen of Hearts**, **Little Jack Horner**, **Little Boy Blue**, **Tom the Piper's Son**, and **Ride a Cock Horse**. The last two were designed for Tom Smith's Ltd. These are the latest in a long line of sets made for Tom Smith since 1973, the first being 'Animate' and the others being 'Safari Park', 'Circus Animals', 'British Wildlife', 'Farmyard', 'Survival', 'Wildlife', 'Family Pets', 'World of Dogs', 'Bird Life' and 'Snow Life'.

Chinese Year of the Dog – A Chinese New Year decanter in a limited edition of 4000 commissioned by Lang Brothers Ltd.

Andy Capp and Flo – Commissioned by C. & S. Collectables in an edition of 1900 (£30-£40/$60-$80). These figures do not have a cigarette. *See 1995 for variation.*

Holly Hedgehog – The second model in the Arthur Hare series commissioned by C. & S. Collectables in a limited edition of 2000 originally selling for £19.95/$40 (£20-£30/$40-$60).

Scooby Doo – Commissioned by G. & G. Collectables in a limited edition of 2000, with each piece being numbered (£40-£50/$80-$100).

Santa on a Sleigh – Produced as a private commission for Keenan Antiques of the U.S.A. in a limited number of 2000 pieces (£15-£20/$30-$40).

Bell's Christmas Decanters – For United Distillers. The U.K. market decanter (£40-£60/$80-$120). The South African market (£220-£280/$440-$560).

1995

Andy Capp and Flo – Commissioned by C. & S. Collectables were issued in an special edition of 100 (£60-£70/$120-$140). This edition was only on sale at the Motor Cycle Museum Wade Fair and differs to that issued in 1994 in that both figures have a cigarette.

Big Bad Wolf and the Three Little Pigs – Available only through the Official International Wade Collectors Club to their members, each model made available with the publication of the Club's quarterly magazine. The first little pig holding a bundle of straw was produced in a limited edition of 1000 (£50-£60/$100-$120), the second little pig, following the complete sell out of the first, was produced in a limited edition of 1250 (£40-£50/$80-$100). The Big Bad Wolf was issued in August in a further increased limited edition of 1500 (£40-£50/$80-$100), due in part to the increasing club membership. By November the final figure, the third Pig, behind a pile of bricks, was released with the Christmas issue, the Wolf having sold out, in a limited edition of 1500 (£40-£50/$80-$100). Each piece selling originally for £15/$30.

Art Deco range – This included five different designs on earthenware pitchers, mugs and vases. The designs are called **Nouvelle**, **Japanese Garden**, **Orange Grove**, **Sunburst** and **Paradise**.

The Bear Ambitions – Miniature series of six bears that were brought out following the Bear Ambitions Collector Teapot range. In the range are **Artistic Edward**, **Admiral Sam**, **Locomotive Joe**, **Beatrice the Ballerina**, **Musical Marco** and **Alex the Aviator** (£2-£3/$4-$6 each).

The Grey Haired Rabbit – A limited edition of 1250 commissioned by UK International Fairs and only available at the June Wade Collectors Fair. At the previous Birmingham UK Fair it had been proposed that a model of a Pony would be the model for this fair, all the stall holders at the fair were given an allocation, the rest then being available to the general public (£40-£50/$80-$100).

Nennie – The first in a proposed series of four Scottie dogs, produced as a private commission for Ficol with a unique backstamp (£25-£35/$50-$70).

The Law and Order Set – The Prisoner. The fourth in a limited edition set commissioned by Elaine and Adrian Crumpton, issued in 2000 pieces. At only

$2^{3}/_{4}$ inches high this was the smallest in the set, the tallest being the Policeman at $3^{5}/_{8}$ inches high, but again as with the Policeman there are two versions of this model. The more common one has black hair (£15-£20/$30-$40) and the rarer one brown hair (£30-£35/$60-$70).

Felicity Squirrel – This was the third piece in the Arthur Hare series commissioned by C. & S. Collectables. It was produced in a limited edition of 1500 in all. I say in all because of the 1500 edition 1250 were produced in grey, marked C. & S. Collectables and 250 were marked 'Collector's Corner'. There were also 250 models produced in red, available at the Dunstable Fair in 1996, of which 6 had the 'Collector's Corner' mark, being made as special presentation pieces not for sale. The grey models are currently selling for £25-£30/$50-$60 and the red for £40-£60/$80-$120.

Holly Hedgehog Mug – Commissioned by C. & S. Collectables, this was produced for the Second Wade Fair at Birmingham, June 1995, in a limited edition of 400 (£10-£15/$20-$30). For the same Fair C. & S. Collectables also issued the first commemorative thimble carrying the same design (£3-£5/$6-$10).

Dougal – A limited edition commission of 2000 figurines by Camtraks. This was to be the first of a series of nostalgic British television and literary characters called Childhoold Favourites. It is available in three variations of face colour and number of base holes. This figure also appears to have been faked and advice from Camtrak's is not to buy a model of Dougal unless it has its two colour certificate and postcard.

Gingerbread Man – Part of a limited number from a proposed Gingerbread Family, commissioned by P. & R. Collectables (£25-£35/$50-$70).

Christmas Puppy – Modelled by Ken Holmes, available as a free gift to subscribers to The Official International Wade Collectors Club (£10-£20/$20-$40).

Rocking Horse Christmas Ornament – Commissioned by Keenan Antiques again as a limited edition (£15-£20/$30-$40).

Hamm's Bear – 'Santa's Helper', in black, commissioned by Silver State Specialities in a limited edition of 2000 (£30-£50/$60-$100 each).

Edward Bear Money Box – Commissioned by Marks & Spencers and sold filled with chocolate coins (£8-£10/$15-$20).

Scrappy Doo – Produced as a companion to Scooby Doo, commissioned by G. & C. Collectables in a limited edition of 2000 (£35-£45/$70-$90).

Snow Woman – Produced in a limited edition of 1500 in time for Christmas, selling for £12.50/$25 and only available from the Wade factory with one figure per member. This model also appeared on the 1995 Christmas Card (£30-£40/$60-$80).

Bell's Christmas Decanters – commissioned by United Distillers. 20,000 were produced by Wade for the U.K. market, in a dark green glaze with gold and red decoration. They also produced 13,000 decanters for the South African market in green/cream glaze.

1996

Goldilocks and The Three Bears – A limited edition series available only to member collectors via the Wade Collectors Club. The first piece being **Mummy Bear** that was originally issued as a limited edition of 1500. Later, however, the Vice President of Wade decided to increase the issue to 2000, at first, finally deciding on 2500. This decision was taken due to the massive demand for such figures from an ever increasing number of club members, but also because members were ordering several at a time. Another reason was to stop the highly inflated prices on the secondary market that developed as soon as the issue was sold out. After all that the second figure, **Daddy Bear**, was issued in a limited edition of 2750, with one of the new rules now coming into effect, namely one figure per member. In the Autumn, 1996, **Goldilocks**, the third in the series was issued in a limited edition of 2750 and finally in November the last figure, **Baby Bear** was released, again in a limited edition of 2750. It should be noted that Daddy Bear and Goldilocks had not sold out, a small number of pieces still being available at the time Baby Bear was issued (£15-£20/$30-$50 each).

The Smiling Frog – A limited edition of 1250 commissioned by U.K. Fairs Ltd and available only at the U.K. Wade Collectors Fair in April. Due to a queue of about 1300 people waiting to get in by 9.00am, it was decided to open the fair half an hour early at 10.00am. By 10.45am the whole edition of the Smiling Frog had sold out (£40-£50/$80-$100).

Westie – A West Highland Terrier, produced in a limited edition of 3000 to be sold only at the first Wade Collectors Club Fair held in America at the Red Lion Hotel, Seattle Airport, on 6th and 7th July 1996. This was produced with a special 'Seattle' fair backstamp (£15-£20/$30-$40).

Miniature Seattle Mug – Commissioned by Keenan Antiques in a limited edition of 500 and sold at the Seattle Wade Fair (£3-£5/$6-$10).

Whimbles – C. & S. Collectables commissioned two pieces, the first to celebrate the success of the **International Wade Collectors Club**, bearing the club logo, issued in a limited edition of 1000, and the second to commemorate the first **U.S.A. Wade Collectors Fair, Seattle**, organised by Wade in association with Jim Beam. This featured the Seattle Space Needle and was produced in a limited edition of 500 available at the Fair. Another Whimble produced by C. & S. Collectables was based on the front of their own shop, **Spooners**, issued in a limited edition of 1000 (£3-£5/$6-$10).

Hamm's Bear – **'Santa's Helper'**, again commissioned by Silver State Specialities in a limited edition of 1200 coloured brown (£30-£50/$60-$100). Another commission was a special model for the Seattle Fair, the word 'Seattle' on a blue cap worn by the bear. This was issued in a limited edition of 2000 (£30/50/$60-$100).

Timid Mouse – Commissioned by U.K. Fairs and produced for the Dunstable Collectors Fair. This piece was issued in a limited edition of 2000, with 1750 being available on the day of the fair and 250 reserved for overseas collectors.

Gaffer Money Box – Commissioned by Tetley G.B. (£50-£60/$100-$120). This was not the only item produced for Tetley during this year, a salt shaker modelled as Sydney and a pepper shaker modelled as the Gaffer (£20-£30/$40-$60).

Mr Punch and Judy – commissioned by Sue and Peggy, designed by Ken Holmes, **Punch** was the first of the figures to be introduced in a limited edition of 2000. This also had a special mark of a Corgi above the Wade logo (£41/$80).

Scottie Dog – available to Official Wade Club members only, together with a new idea for members, of a Scottie Dog pin. The Scottie Dog was later to be named **Smudger**, following a 'Name that dog . . .' competition.

Red Felicity Squirrel – This piece was commissioned by C. & S. Collectables in a limited edition of 250 and available at the Dunstable U.K. Wade Fair. Also available at the same stand were a limited edition of 250 **Commemorative Mugs** (£8-£10/$16-$20) with the International Wade Club Logo as well as 500 **Commemorative Wade Fair Whimbles** (£3-£5/$6-$10) depicting **Arthur Hare**.

The Snow Children – The final piece of the Christmas special snow people series was issued in time for Christmas 1996, although the deadline for orders was extended to December 31st from October 31st due to a slight glitch in sending out the Autumn edition of the Official International Wade Collectors Club magazine. By February 1997 the whole limited edition of 2500 pieces, increased from 1500, had sold out, somewhat faster than the original Wade Limited Editions promotion Welcome Home, Fireside Friend and Togetherness (£20-£30/$40-$60).

Betty Boop – Commissioned by C. & S. Collectables and designed by Ken Holmes. This figure was produced with a red dress (1500) and blue dress (500), the latter being split evenly for sale at the Wisconsin USA Wade Fair in July 1997 and the Wade Swap Meet in Arundel in August 1997.

The Flintstones – Produced by Wade Ceramics Ltd and commissioned by U.K. International Ceramics Ltd. this set was issued in a limited edition of 1500 for each of the six pieces. The first two figures issued were **Fred and Wilma**, each 4½ inches high, to be followed by **Betty** and **Barney** and then later mid-way through 1997, **Bam-Bam** and **Pebbles**.

Rupert the Bear – the second in the Childhood Favourites commissioned by Camtrak. In an edition size of 2000 this was split into two variants a green base (1900) and a gold base(100).

1997
Pantomime Series – Following on from the Goldilocks and the Three Bears the new series for Collectors Club Members only, launched in 1997, was based on pantomime characters, modelled by Ken Holmes. The first was **Pantomime Horse**, to be followed by **Dick Whittington's Cat** and two other pieces. This was issued in a rather massive, by Wade's standards, limited edition of 4000 on a first come first served basis, one per member.

Dracula – Commissioned by Nexus/Wade in a limited edition of 2500 (Wade sold 1250 in matt, Nexus sold 1250 in a gloss finish). This model at 10³/₄inches high is one of the largest figures ever produced by Wade and came with a specially designed presentation box. The figure, based on Christopher Lee's characterisation of Dracula, commemorates the fortieth anniversary of Hammer Studio's first horror film.

Popeye – Commissioned by David Trower Enterprises, Popeye was the first figure in a whole set of the Popeye collection.

Judy – Following on the success of their first figure, **Mr Punch**, Peggy Gamble and Sue Styles issued the companion figure **Judy** in March 1997. This figure was produced in a limited edtion of 2000 with the first 1800 produced in blue to match Mr Punch, the rest of the 200 figures to be issued in a colour to be announced later. Each of these figures carries Peggy and Sue's distinctive backstamp of a Corgi together with the usual Wade backstamp.

Yogi Bear – This figure was the first to be released in a limited edtion of 1500 by G. & G. Collectables with **Boo Boo** to follow.

Seal Pup – This model was introduced as part of the 'enrol a friend' scheme whereby both the member and their new member friend would receive a Seal Pup figurine.

The Smurfs – As I write this is a set of the Smurfs and a figure of Gargamel are about to appear in Wade porcelain.

Kangaroo – Produced by Wade Ceramics and commissioned by U.K. Fairs Ltd. Issued in a limited edition of 1500 and available only at the fourth U.K. Official Wade Collectors Fair, to take place at Trentham Gardens, in April. As an added bonus to overseas collectors a special edition of 150 Kangaroos were to be issued with overseas backstamp, but only available to those who bought the previous years Timid Mouse.

Edward Fox – The next model in the Arthur Hare series commissioned by C. & S. Collectables was only available at the Trentham Wade Fair in a limited edition of 1000, and already selling at 120% of its purchase price.

Paddington – the third in the Childhood Favourites commissioned by Camtrak. again in an edition size of 2001. This is split into three variants: a grey cobbled base (1900), gold base(100) and a one off gold base.

Editions to come
Camtracks
50th Anniversary Sooty and Sweep (Spring/Summer 1998)
Childhoold Favourites Christmas Special No 1 Rupert & Snowman (1997)
Childhoold Favourites Christmas Special No 2 Paddington Bear (1998)
G & G Collectables
Mr Jinks, Pixie and Dixie, Huckleberry Hound
C. & S. Collectables
Betty Boop Classic and Betty Boop Christmas Surprise

Faults, Fakes and Imitations

The fact that this chapter is even here is a sign that Wade has reached the dizzy heights of collectability. One could even say respectability, now that a couple of the major London auction rooms have included special sections of Wade and related items amongst the pages of their expensive illustrated catalogues.

Over the years there are certain anomalies that are bound to affect the end product of many production pieces, especially when they are produced in vast quantities. In other words you will always find variations in shape, when the metal die has to be renewed for example or when comparing the first items out of a mould compared to the later ones. In the moulding process itself, when the model is ejected, small bits might get left in the mould. Glaze colouring can also vary, after all humans mix the ingredients, so what can you expect? Once a certain model has been in production for a few months a decision might be made to slightly alter the colouring.

Faults and variations are all very well and often acceptable, once you have satisfied yourself of the problem and feel the price is still fair. What is totally unacceptable is the outright faking of old and even new pieces. The most recent problems seem to surround the model of the Policeman, commissioned by Elaine and Adrian Crumpton in 1993. There are two legitimate versions of this figure, one with a painted face and another with the helmet over the eyes, each produced in numbered limited editions. The fakes would appear to be of the model with the painted face and have a yellow badge and either a pale blue or black uniform. Of the older pieces the Noddy and Big Ears set seem to be on the market in fairly large numbers, the fake models are slightly larger and have been made of a soft body rather than the hard porcelain of the originals. They have also been decorated with bright on-glaze colours instead of slightly more subdued underglaze colours.

The most reported and widely known fakes, made to deliberately deceive collectors, are the Shire Horse and the model of the Swan as seen in set ten of the early Whimsies. Even to the untrained eye the differences are fairly apparent, the fakes having a thicker sugary glaze which alone makes the definition of the models appear crude, but the modelling is crude enough already with a badly defined body, misshapen hoofs and rather a fat head on the horse and a similar lack of detail on the swan. You will find that the Shire Horse even has trouble standing on a hard flat surface. Other such items with similar defects are the Easter Bunny, Bo-Peep and the Kissing Rabbits. The former two are very much reduced in size, while the Kissing Rabbits have features at different angles such as the ears.

In recent years reports have been circulating of other reproductions including: Nurseries, Humpty-Humpty, Little Bo-Peep and Little Red Riding Hood. With these it would appear that the general use of colour is either wrong and/or too bright.

Doubts have also been reported about the reproductions of models such as Dougal, commissioned by Camtrak in 1995, Friar Tuck commissioned by Ian Warner and Mike Posgay and a recent series of Circus Figurines, commissioned by Red Rose Tea for sale in the U.S. only. These models are either being sold far too cheaply, without certificates or in the wrong country. So beware.

In your travels searching for pieces of Wade to add to your collection you will also come across some interesting reproductions. The Studio Szeiler versions of some of the Wade animals. such as Mrs Duck (illustrated in the text), tortoises, etc, are always marked, where possible with the Szeiler mark. These products are the work of the Hungarian immigrant Joseph Szeiler who worked for Wade as a modeller for a number of years before setting up his own studio in Burslem. There are also some direct imitations of Jessie Van Hallen's figures made at the Howard Pottery under the Brentleigh trade name, which are sometimes not marked. Once handled the differences are obvious, being cruder in body and decoration.

This is just another chapter to be added to the story of Wade. It's a sad fact, but true, that having reached this stage you can be sure that Wade products are now officially highly collectable.

Watch out for these genuine collectors pieces below . . .

Smiling Frog made exclusively for UK Fairs in 1996 in a limited edition of 1750 now fetches £35/$70 compared with the original selling price of £16/$30. The model is 4 inches in size.

Felix the Cat made exclusively for UK International Ceramics Ltd in a limited edition of 1500 retails at £38/$75.

Australian Kangaroo produced for UK Fairs Limited in 1997 for the UK Wade Fairs in England, in a limited edition of 1500. The model is 4½ inches in heigh. Issued at a price of £18/$35, current value is now around £35/$70.

Price Guide

Animals

From the late 1920s George Wade produced cellulose-finished animal figures of medium size. In a similar fashion to the celluose figurines, these lost their popularity due to the unstable nature of the cellulose and were replaced in the early 1930s with a line of slip cast, porcelain figure with an underglaze finish, and if applied carried the mark of number 4, seen in the Marks and Backstamps section. 1935 saw George Wade introduce a range that consisted of new models as well as some using the cellulose moulds. The new mould animals were based on wood carvings by Faust Lang, were of extremely high qualityand so expensive, and production was only stopped due to the outbreak of war in 1939. These models carry the 'Wade England' backstamp along with the name of the figure and occasionally year of manufacture. The factory produced a set of bird figures, also based on Lang designs, but due to the lateness of their introduction they weren't marketed fully until after the war, when Wade Heath obtained the moulds and produced them until the mid 1950s.

Wade Heath produced a set of oranmental comical animal figures from the late 1930s until, again war stopped production and there is no record that these were continued once hostilities ceased. After the war Wade Heath obtained some moulds from George Wade and along with some of their own moulds produced a range of animal figures until the mid 1950s.

Abbreviations in price guide
E + Early   L = Late   M = Mid

Name	Size	Production	Market Price	
Bears				
Bear	1⅝x2½	1930-1939	£150-£200	$300-$400
Brown Bear (F. Lang)	9½	1939	£600-£900	$1200-$1800
Polar Bear (F. Lang)	7¼	1935-1939	£1200-£1500	$2400-$3000
Polar Bear (Ireland)		1978-1980	£300-£400	$600-$800
Koala Bear (Ireland)	7	1978-1980	£300-£400	$600-$800
Bears (Panda)				
Baby Panda	1½x2¼	1930-1939	£200-£300	$400-$600
Giant Panda (F. Lang)	7½	1939	£1000-£1200	$2000-$2400
Birds				
Budgerigar (F. Lang)	6¾	1935-1939	£400-£600	$800-$1200
Budgerigar (F. Lang)	8	L30s-M50s	£400-£600	$400-$1200
Cheeky Duckling		1937-1939	£120-£180	$240-$360
Chick	1¾	1930-1939	£100-£150	$200-$300
Cockatoo (F. Lang)	5¾	1935-1939	£500-£700	$1000-$1400

Name	Size	Production	Market Price	
Cockatoo (F. Lang)	6	L30s-M50s	£500-£700	$1000-$1400
Drake and Daddy	$3\frac{1}{8}$x2	1930-1939	£120-£160	$240-$320
Drake and Daddy	$3\frac{1}{8}$x2	1948-1959	£100-£150	$200-$300
Duck	$1\frac{5}{8}$x$1\frac{3}{4}$	1930-1939	£100-£150	$200-$300
Duck	$1\frac{1}{2}$x$1\frac{1}{4}$	1930-1939	£100-£150	$200-$300
Duck	$1\frac{1}{2}$x$1\frac{1}{4}$	1930-1939	£100-£150	$200-$300
Duck	$2\frac{3}{4}$x$2\frac{1}{8}$	1930-1939	£100-£150	$200-$300
Duck	$1\frac{3}{4}$x$3\frac{1}{8}$	1930-1939	£100-£150	$200-$300
Duck	3x$3\frac{1}{8}$	1930-1939	£100-£150	$200-$300
Duck	3x$2\frac{1}{8}$	1930-1939	£100-£150	$200-$300
Duck	2x$\frac{7}{8}$	1930-1939	£100-£150	$200-$300
(Long Necked - Head up)				
Duck	2x$\frac{3}{4}$	1930-1939	£100-£125	$200-$250
(Long Necked – Head down)				
Duck	2x$\frac{3}{4}$	1948-1959	£100-£125	$200-$250
(Long Necked – Head down)				
Duck	2x$\frac{7}{8}$	1948-1959	£100-£125	$200-$250
(Long Necked – Head up)				
Goldfinch (Head down)	4	L30s-M50s	£200-£300	$400-$600
Goldfinch (Head up)	4	L30s-M50s	£200-£300	$400-$600
Grebe (F. Lang)	$9\frac{1}{4}$	1935-1939	£600-£800	$1200-$1600
Hawk	$13\frac{1}{2}$	Post-war	(not available)	
Heron (F. Lang)	7	L30s-M50s	£500-£700	$1000-$1400
Long Necked Duck	$3\frac{3}{4}$x$1\frac{3}{8}$	1930-1939	£200-£300	$400-$600
Mallard	$3\frac{5}{8}$x$3\frac{1}{2}$	1930-1939	£200-£300	$400-$600
Owl	$5\frac{1}{2}$	c1940	£400-£500	$800-$1000
Parrot (F. Lang)	$10\frac{1}{4}$	1935-1939	£700-£1000	$1400-$2000
Pelican	5	L30s-M50s	£200-£300	$400-$600
Seagull	1	1948-1959	£100-£150	$200-$300
Toucan		1930s	£180-£220	$360-$440
Two Budgerigars (F. Lang)	$7\frac{3}{4}$	1935-1939	£700-£900	$1400-$1800
Woodpecker (F. Lang)	6	L30s-M50s	£400-£600	$800-$1200
Birds (Connoisseurs Collection)				
Bullfinch	$7\frac{1}{4}$	1978-1982	£200-£300	$400-$600
Coal Tit	$5\frac{3}{4}$	1978-1982	£200-£300	$400-$600
Goldcrest	$5\frac{1}{4}$	1978-1982	£200-£300	$400-$600
Nuthatch	$5\frac{1}{2}$	1978-1982	£200-£300	$400-$600
Robin	5	1978-1982	£200-£300	$400-$600
Wren	$4\frac{1}{2}$	1978-1982	£200-£300	$400-$600
Bearded Tit	$6\frac{1}{2}$	1980-1982	£200-£300	$400-$600
Dipper	$5\frac{1}{2}$	1980-1982	£200-£300	$400-$600
Kingfisher	7	1980-1982	£200-£300	$400-$600
Redstart	7	1980-1982	£200-£300	$400-$600
Woodpecker	$6\frac{1}{2}$	1980-1982	£200-£300	$400-$600
Yellow Wagtail	$4\frac{1}{2}$	1980-1982	£200-£300	$400-$600

Name	Size	Production	Market Price	
Birds (Quack Quack Family)				
Dack	$1\frac{1}{2}$x$1\frac{1}{8}$	1948-1959	£150-£175	$300-$350
Dilly	$1\frac{1}{2}$x$1\frac{1}{8}$	1948-1959	£150-£175	$300-$350
Mr Duck	$2\frac{1}{2}$x$1\frac{1}{2}$	1948-1959	£125-£150	$250-$300
Mrs Duck	$2\frac{1}{2}$x$1\frac{1}{2}$	1948-1959	£125-£150	$250-$300
Camels				
Camel (F Lang?)	$7\frac{3}{4}$x$6\frac{3}{4}$	1935-1939	£700-£900	$1400-$1800
Cats				
Cat	$1\frac{1}{2}$x$2\frac{1}{8}$	1930-1939	£75-£100	$150-$200
Cat	$1\frac{1}{8}$x$2\frac{7}{8}$	1930-1939	£75-£100	$150-$200
Cat	$1\frac{1}{4}$x$1\frac{3}{4}$	1930-1939	£75-£100	$150-$200
Cat	$1\frac{1}{2}$x$2\frac{1}{8}$	1930-1939	£75-£100	$150-$200
Cat	1x$2\frac{3}{4}$	1930-1939	£75-£100	$150-$200
Cat	1x$2\frac{3}{4}$	1930-1939	£75-£100	$150-$200
Cat	$1\frac{1}{2}$	1948-1959	£60-£80	$120-$160
Cat	$1\frac{1}{2}$	1948-1959	£60-£80	$120-$160
Cat	$1\frac{1}{2}$	1948-1959	£60-£80	$120-$160
Cat	$1\frac{1}{2}$	1948-1959	£60-£80	$120-$160
Cat	$1\frac{1}{2}$	1948-1959	£60-£80	$120-$160
Cows				
Calf	$2\frac{3}{8}$x$1\frac{1}{4}$	1930-1939	£200	$400
Deers				
Deer	$1\frac{1}{8}$x$1\frac{1}{4}$	1930-1939	£120-£150	$240-$300
Deer	$2\frac{1}{2}$x$1\frac{3}{4}$	1930-1939	£130-£160	$260-$320
Stag	$8\frac{3}{4}$	1935-1939	£700-£900	$1400-$1800
Dogs				
Airedale	7x8	1927-1937	£150-£250	$300-$500
Alsatian	$10\frac{1}{4}$x18	1927-1937	£140-£160	$280-$300
Alsatian	$4\frac{3}{4}$x$8\frac{3}{4}$	1927-1937	£150-£250	$300-$500
Begging Puppy	$3\frac{1}{8}$x$1\frac{3}{4}$	1930-1939	£120-£130	$240-$260
Borzoi	12x$12\frac{1}{2}$	1927-1937	£500-£700	$1000-$1400
Dachshund	$3\frac{1}{8}$x$1\frac{1}{2}$	1930-1939	£150-£200	$300-$400
Dalmation	$8\frac{3}{4}$x$12\frac{1}{2}$	1927-1937	£300-£500	$600-$1000
Pongo	$5\frac{5}{8}$x$5\frac{1}{8}$	1937-1939	£80-£100	$160-$200
Pongo	$5\frac{1}{8}$x$4\frac{5}{8}$	1937-1939	£60-£80	$120-$160
Pongo	$4\frac{5}{8}$x4	1937-1939	£40-£60	$80-$120
Scottie	$4\frac{3}{4}$x$6\frac{1}{4}$	1927-1937	£200-£300	$240-$600
Setter	6x$9\frac{3}{4}$	1927-1937	£200-£300	$240-$600
Setter	$3\frac{1}{2}$x$2\frac{1}{4}$	1930-1939	£100-£120	$200-$240
Setter	$3\frac{1}{2}$	1948-1959	£120-£150	$240-$300
Sitting Scottie		1937-1939	£60-£80	$120-$160
Spaniel	$5\frac{1}{2}$x5	1927-1937	£250-£300	$500-$600
Spaniel (Playful Puppy)	$2\frac{1}{2}$x$5\frac{1}{2}$	1927-1937	£200-£250	$400-$500
Terrier	7x8	1927-1937	£250-£300	$500-$600
Terrier		1937-1939	£60-£80	$120-$160
Walking Scottie		1937-1939	£80-£100	$160-$200

Name	Size	Production	Market Price	
Dogs (Championship Dogs)				
Afghan Hound	3x3³/₈	1975-1981	£35-£55	$70-$110
Cocker Spaniel	2⁷/₈x3⁵/₈	1975-1981	£35-£55	$70-$110
Collie	3¹/₈x4	1975-1981	£35-£55	$70-$110
English Setter	2³/₄x4¹/₈	1975-1981	£35-£55	$70-$110
Old English Sheepdog	3¹/₈x3	1975-1981	£35-£55	$70-$110
Dogs and Puppies				
Alsatian (Adult)	2¹/₂x2³/₈	1969-1982	£8-£12	$15-$25
Alsatian (Puppy)	1¹/₄x2	1969-1982	£8-£12	$15-$25
Alsatian (Puppy)	1³/₄x1⁵/₈	1969-1982	£8-£12	$15-$25
Cairn (Adult)	2¹/₂x2³/₄	1969-1982	£8-£12	$15-$25
Cairn (Puppy)	1¹/₂x1³/₈	1969-1982	£8-£12	$15-$25
Cairn (Puppy)	1³/₈x2	1969-1982	£8-£12	$15-$25
Corgi (Adult)	2¹/₄x2¹/₄	1979-1982	£15-£25	$30-$50
Corgi (Puppy)	1⁵/₈x1³/₈	1979-1982	£10-£20	$20-$40
Corgi (Puppy)	1¹/₈	1979-1982	£10-£20	$20-$40
Red Setter (Adult)	2¹/₄x2⁷/₈	1979-1982	£8-£12	$15-$25
Red Setter (Puppy)	1¹/₂x1³/₄	1979-1982	£8-£12	$15-$25
Red Setter (Puppy)	1¹/₂x1³/₄	1979-1982	£8-£12	$15-$25
Yorkshire Terrier (Adult)	2¹/₈x1⁵/₈	1979-1982	£20-£40	$40-$80
Yorkshire Terrier (Puppy)	1³/₈x1¹/₂	1979-1982	£15-£25	$30-$50
Yorkshire Terrier (Puppy)	1¹/₂x1¹/₄	1979-1982	£15-£25	$30-$50
Donkeys				
Cheerful Charlie	4³/₈x2¹/₈	1948-1959	£140-$170	$280-$340
Doleful Dan	4³/₈x2¹/₈	1948-1959	£140-$170	$280-$340
Donkey	1⁷/₈x1¹/₂	1930-1939	£150-£180	$300-$380
Foal	1¹/₂x1¹/₄	1930-1939	£120-£150	$240-$300
Elephants				
Elephant	2x2¹/₂	1930-1939	£150-£200	$300-$400
Elephant	2	1948-1959	£100-£130	$200-$260
Elephant (Ireland)		1978-1980	£300-£400	$600-$800
Jumbo Jim		1937-1939	£100-£130	$200-$260
Ermines				
Ermine (F. Lang)	9¹/₂x3	1935-1939	£1200-£1800	$2400-$3600
Giraffes				
Giraffe (F. Lang)	3x4	1935-1939	£300-£400	$600-$800
Goats				
Chamois Kid	5¹/₄x3¹/₄	1935-1939	£400-£600	$800-$1200
Ibex	2¹/₄x2¹/₄	1930-1939	£200-£250	$400-$500
Horse Set				
Foal	1⁷/₈x2	1974-1978	£10-£15	$20-$30
Foal	1³/₈x2	1974-1978	£10-£15	$20-$30
Horse	2³/₄x3	1974-1978	£10-£15	$20-$30
Foal	1¹/₂x1⁵/₈	1978-1981	£35-£45	$70-$90
Foal	1¹/₄x1⁷/₈	1978-1981	£35-£45	$70-$90
Horse	2¹/₂x2³/₄	1978-1981	£35-£45	$70-$90

Name	Size	Production	Market Price	
Horses				
Dartmoor Pony	4⅞x4¼	1935-1939	£200-£250	$400-$500
Dartmoor Pony	4x4	1935-1939	£200-£250	$400-$500
Foal	2½x2½	1930-1939	£150-£200	$300-$400
Foal	2x2¼	1930-1939	£150-£200	$300-$400
Horse	7¾x6¾	1935-1939	£500-£700	$1000-$1400
Hippopotamus				
Hippopotamus	1⅜x4½	1930s	£300-£400	$600-$800
Lions				
Lion Cub				
– Paw down (F. Lang)	5¼x7¼	1935-1939	£1200-£1500	$2400-$3000
– Paw up (F. Lang)	5¼x7¼	1935-1939	£1200-£1500	$2400-$3000
Lion (Ireland)		1978-1980	£300-£400	$600-$800
Monkeys				
Capuchin (F. Lang)	10	1935-1939	£800-£1000	$1600-$2000
Monkey	1⅛x¾	1930-1939	£150-£200	$300-$500
Monkey	2½x2	1930-1939	£200-£350	$400-$700
Otters				
Otter (F. Lang)	4x10¾	1935-1939	£800-£1000	$1600-$2000
Panthers				
Panther (F. Lang)	8x5	1935-1939	£800-£1000	$1600-$2000
Penguin Family				
Benny	2x1	1948-1959	£100-£150	$200-$300
Mr Penguin	3½x1½	1948-1959	£80-£120	$160-$240
Mrs Penguin	3x1½	1948-1959	£80-£120	$160-$240
Penny	2x1	1948-1959	£100-£150	$200-$300
Penguins				
Penguin	2¾x2¼	1930-1939	£150-£200	$300-$400
Pig Family				
Boy Pig			£150-£160	$300-$320
Girl Pig			£150-£160	$300-$320
Mr Pig			£60-£70	$120-$140
Mrs Pig			£60-£70	$120-$140
Rabbit Family				
Fluff	1½x1⅛	1948-1959	£120-£150	$240-$300
Mr Rabbit	3½x1½	1948-1959	£80-£120	$160-$240
Mrs Rabbit	3½x1½	1948-1959	£80-£120	$160-$240
Puff	1½x1⅛	1948-1959	£120-£150	$240-$300
Rabbits				
Bunny	⅞x1⅛	1930-1939	£30-£50	$60-$100
Bunny	⅞x1	1948-1959	£30-£50	$60-$100
Crouching Rabbit		1937-1939	£80-£120	$160-$240
Double Bunnies	⅞x1	1930-1939	£55-£75	$110-$150
Double Bunnies	1¼x1¾	1930-1939	£60-£80	$120-$160
Double Bunnies	1⅝x2¾	1930-1939	£70-£90	$140-$180
Double Bunnies	⅞	1948-1959	£50-£70	$100-$140

Name	Size	Production	Market Price	
Double Bunnies	$1\frac{5}{8}$x1	1948-1959	£70-£90	$140-$180
Kissing Bunnies	$2\frac{1}{2}$x$2\frac{3}{4}$	1930-1939	£60-£70	$120-$140
Kissing Bunnies	$2\frac{1}{2}$x$2\frac{3}{4}$	1948-1959	£70-£90	$140-$180
Laughing Rabbit	$5\frac{5}{8}$x$\frac{5}{8}$	1937-1939	£80-£120	$160-$240
Laughing Rabbit	$6\frac{3}{8}$x$2\frac{7}{8}$	1937-1939	£100-£150	$200-$300
Laughing Rabbit	7x3	1937-1939	£120-£180	$240-$360
Little Laughing Bunny	$2\frac{1}{2}$x$1\frac{1}{2}$	L40s-E50s	£0	$0
Old Buck	$6\frac{5}{8}$x$5\frac{5}{8}$	1937-1939	£150-£200	$300-$400
Rabbit (miniature)		1937-1939	£50-£60	$100-$120
Rabbit (small)		1937-1939	£60-£70	$120-$140
Rabbit (medium)		1937-1939	£70-£90	$140-$180
Rabbit (large)		1937-1939	£100-£120	$200-$240
Standing Rabbit	$2\frac{5}{8}$x$1\frac{3}{8}$	1930-1939	£60-£90	$120-£180
Standing Rabbit	$2\frac{1}{2}$	1948-1959	£60-£90	$120-£180
Razorback				
Razorback	5x8		£600-£800	$1200-$1600
Rhinoceros				
Rhino (Ireland)		1978-1980	£300-£400	$600-$800
Rhinoceros Ashtray	$8\frac{1}{4}$	1962	£250-£300	$500-$600
Rhinoceros Ashtray	$5\frac{1}{2}$	1962	£250-£300	$500-$600
Sealions				
Sealion		1960	£120-£150	$240-$300
Sheep				
Lamb	$2\frac{1}{8}$x2	1930-1939	£125-£175	$250-$350
Lamb	2x$2\frac{3}{8}$	1930-1939	£125-£175	$250-$350
Lamb	2x$2\frac{3}{8}$	1930-1939	£125-£175	$250-$350
Lamb	$1\frac{1}{2}$x$1\frac{1}{4}$	1930-1939	£125-£175	$250-$350
Lamb	2x$2\frac{3}{8}$	1948-1959	£100-£120	$200-$240
Lamb	2	1948-1959	£100-£120	$200-$240
Squirrels				
Squirrel	$1\frac{1}{2}$	1948-1959	£60-£80	$120-$160
Squirrel	$1\frac{5}{8}$x$2\frac{1}{8}$	1930-1939	£80-£100	$160-£200
Squirrel	$2\frac{1}{2}$x$2\frac{1}{2}$	1930-1939	£125-£175	$250-$350
Squirrel		1937-1939	£125-£175	$250-$350
Survival		1991	£2000-£3500	$4000-$7000
Tortoise Family				
'Slow Fe' Baby Tortoise	$1\frac{1}{4}$x3	1969-1970	£45-£75	$90-$150
Baby Tortoise	$1\frac{1}{4}$x3	1960	£10-£12	$20-$24
Baby Tortoise	$\frac{7}{8}$x2	1960	£10-£12	$20-$24
Extra Large Tortoise	$2\frac{3}{8}$x6	1973	£50-£70	$100-$140
Large Tortoise	$2\frac{3}{4}$x4	1958	£20-£25	$40-$50
Tortoise	$1\frac{1}{4}$x3	1930s	£300-£400	$600-$800
Walrus				
Walrus (Ireland)	6	1978-1980	£300-£400	$600-$800
World of Survival				
African Elephant	6x10	1978-1982	£250-£350	$500-$700

Name	Size	Production	Market Price	
African Lion	4½x8	1978-1982	£175-£220	$350-$440
American Bison	4½x8	1978-1982	£175-£220	$350-$440
Black Rhinoceros	4½x9½	1978-1982	£175-£220	$350-$440
Polar Bear	4½x8½	1978-1982	£175-£220	$350-$440
Tiger	3½x8	1978-1982	£250-£350	$500-$700
African (Cape) Buffalo	5x9¼	1980-1982	£350-£450	$700-$900
American Brown Bear	4x5½	1980-1982	£300-£400	$600-$800
American Cougar (Puma)	4x9	1980-1982	£275-£320	$550-$640
Gorilla	5½x5¾	1980-1982	£300-£400	$600-$800
Harp Seal & Pup	3¾x9	1980-1982	£350-£450	$700-$900
Hippopotamus	4½x10	1980-1982	£275-£320	$550-$640

Aquarium

This consists of a set of six models and were commissioned from George Wade by King British Aquarium Accessories Ltd. Equal number of each model was produced over a three to four year production period. The Seahorse and the Snail are the most difficult to find.

Bridge	2¾x3⅝	1974-1990	£40-£50	$80-$100
Diver	2¾x1	1974-1990	£20-£30	$40-$60
Lighthouse	3x1¾	1974-1990	£35-£45	$70-$90
Mermaid	2½x2¼	1974-1990	£20-£30	$40-$60
Sea Horse		1974-1990	£100-£120	$200-$240
Snail		1974-1990	£80-£100	$160-$200

Characters from Film & Literature

Nothing is more collectable than that which is liable to provoke happy memories from the past. Therefore characters that appear in films, first in the cinema and then on television, are likely to prove most popular, and topping the list are those that have ever-lasting appeal. Here Walt Disney has an unchallenging lead for cinema, and Hanna-Barbera for television characters.

Mickey Mouse		1934	£1200-£1500	$2400-$3000
Disney (Blow-Ups)				
Am	5½	1961-1965	£100-£120	$200-$240
Bambi		1961-1965	£70-£90	$140-$180
Dachie	5½	1961-1965	£300-£350	$600-$700
Jock		1961-1965	£300-£350	$600-$700
Lady		1961-1965	£120-£150	$240-$300
Scamp	4⅛x5	1961-1965	£100-£120	$200-$240
Si	5½x5	1961-1965	£100-£120	$200-$240
Thumper	5½	1961-1965	£160-£180	$320-$360
Tramp		1961-1965	£190-£210	$380-$420
Trusty	5½	1961-1965	£120-£140	$240-$280

Name	*Size*	*Production*	*Market Price*	
Disneys				
Big Mama	1¾x1¾	1981-1985	£15-£30	$30-$60
Chief	1⅞x1	1981-1985	£15-£30	$30-$60
Copper	1⅝x1½	1981-1985	£15-£30	$30-$60
Peg	1½x1⅝	1981-1985	£15-£30	$30-$60
Tod	1¾x1⅞	1981-1985	£30-£40	$60-$80
Tramp	1⅞x1¼	1981-1985	£30-£40	$60-$80
Bambi	1½x1⅜	1981-1985	£15-£30	$30-$60
Dachsie	1¾x1½	1981-1985	£15-£30	$30-$60
Jock (Green Tartan)	1½x1	1981-1985	£15-£30	$30-$60
Lady	1½x1⅜	1981-1985	£15-£30	$30-$60
Scamp	1½x1½	1981-1985	£15-£30	$30-$60
Thumper	1⅞x1¼	1981-1985	£15-£30	$30-$60
Hanna-Barbera Cartoon Characters				
Huckleberry Hound	2⅜x1⅛	1959-1960	£50-£60	$100-$120
Mr Jinks	2½x1⅛	1959-1960	£60-£70	$120-$140
Yogi Bear	2½x1⅛	1959-1960	£60-£70	$120-$140
Hatbox (101 Dalmatians)				
Lucky		1961	£45-£55	$90-$110
Rolly	1⅞x1⅜	1961	£45-£55	$90-$110
Sergeant Tibbs	2x1⅝	1961	£45-£55	$90-$110
The Colonel	2x1½	1961	£40-£50	$80-$100
Hatbox (Bambi)				
Bambi	1½x1⅜	1957	£10-£15	$20-$30
Flower	1½x1¾	1957	£25-£30	$50-$60
Thumper	1⅞x1¼	1957	£10-£15	$20-$30
Hatbox (Dumbo)				
Dumbo	1⅜x1⅝	1957	£25-£30	$50-$60
Hatbox (Fantasia)				
Baby Pegasus	1¾x1⅛	1958	£25-£30	$50-$60
Hatbox (Lady and the Tramp)				
Am	1⅞x1	1958	£15-£20	$30-$40
Boris	2⅜x1	1960	£20-£25	$40-$50
Dachie	1¾x1½	1958	£10-£15	$20-$30
Jock	1¾x1⅝	1956	£10-£15	$20-$30
Lady	1½x1¾	1956	£10-£15	$20-$30
Peg	1½x1⅝	1957	£10-£15	$20-$30
Scamp	1½x1½	1957	£10-£15	$20-$30
Si	1⅞x1⅛	1958	£15-£20	$30-$40
Toughy	2x1¼	1960	£30-£35	$60-$70
Tramp	2⅛x1⅞	1956	£25-£30	$50-$60
Trusty	2⅜x1⅜	1956	£10-£15	$20-$30
Hatbox (Sword in the Stone)				
Archimedes		1962	£65-£75	$130-$150
Girl Squirrel		1962	£50-£60	$100-$120
Madam Mim		1962	£90-£100	$180-$200

Name	Size	Production	Market Price	
Merlin as a Caterpillar		1962	£100-£120	$200-$240
Merlin as a Hare	2¼x1⅜	1962	£120-£140	$240-$280
Merlin as a Turtle		1962	£150-£170	$300-$340
Noddy				
Big Ears	2½x1½	1958-1960	£90-£110	$180-$220
Miss Fluffy Cat	2½x1½	1958-1960	£30-£40	$60-$80
Mr Plod	2½x1½	1958-1960	£70-£80	$140-$160
Noddy	2½x1½	1958-1960	£150-£200	$300-$400
Nursery Favourites				
Humpty Dumpty	1⅜x1¾	1972-1981	£10-£20	$20-$40
Jack	2⅞x1⅛	1972-1981	£10-£20	$20-$40
Jill	2⅞x1⅛	1972-1981	£10-£20	$20-$40
Little Jack Horner	1⅞x1¼	1972-1981	£10-£20	$20-$40
Little Miss Muffet	2⅝x1⅞	1972-1981	£10-£20	$20-$40
Mary Had a Little Lamb	2⅞x1⅜	1973-1981	£10-£20	$20-$40
Old King Cole	2½x1⅞	1973-1981	£10-£20	$20-$40
Polly Put the Kettle On	2⅞x1¼	1973-1981	£10-£20	$20-$40
Tom Tom the Piper's Son	2¾x2	1973-1981	£10-£20	$20-$40
Wee Willie Winkie	1¾x1½	1973-1981	£10-£20	$20-$40
Cat and the Fiddle	2⅞x1⅜	1974-1981	£10-£20	$20-$40
Little Boy Blue	2⅞x1⅛	1974-1981	£30-£50	$60-$100
Little Tommy Tucker	3x1⅛	1974-1981	£10-£20	$20-$40
Mary Mary Quite Contrary	2⅞x1⅛	1974-1981	£30-£50	$60-$100
Queen of Hearts	2⅞x1⅞	1974-1981	£10-£20	$20-$40
Goosey Gander	2⅝x1⅛	1976-1981	£70-£100	$140-$200
Little Bo-Beep	2⅞x1⅛	1976-1981	£40-£60	$80-$120
Old Woman Who Lived in a Shoe	2½x2⅛	1976-1981	£60-£80	$120-$160
Puss in Boots	2⅞x1⅛	1976-1981	£30-£50	$60-$100
Three Bears	2⅞x2¼	1976-1981	£40-£60	$80-$120
Nursery Rhymes				
Blynken	2¼x1½	1948-1959	£100-£120	$200-$240
I've a Bear Behind	2¾x1½	1948-1959	£125-£150	$250-$300
Nod	2¾x1½	1948-1959	£100-£120	$200-$240
Wynken	3x1½	1948-1959	£100-£120	$200-$240
Baby Bear	1¾	1948-1959	£200-£250	$400-$500
Father Bear	3½	1948-1959	£200-£225	$400-$500
Goldilocks	4	1948-1959	£200-£225	$400-$500
Mother Bear	3¾	1948-1959	£200-£225	$400-$500
Baker	3⅞	1950-1955	£300-£350	$600-$700
Butcher	3¼	1950-1955	£175-£200	$350-$400
Candlestick Maker	4	1950-1955	£300-£350	$600-$700
Little Jack Horner	2½	1950-1955	£300-£350	$600-$700
Little Miss Muffet	2½	1950-1955	£300-£350	$600-$700
Beggar Man	2½	1950-1959	£120-£150	$240-$300
Poor Man	3	1950-1959	£120-£150	$240-$300

Name	Size	Production	Market Price	
Rich Man	3	1950-1959	£120-£150	$240-$300
Sailor	3	1950-1959	£180-£200	$360-$400
Tailor	2½	1950-1959	£120-£150	$240-$300
Thief	3	1950-1959	£120-£150	$240-$300
Tinker	2½	1950-1959	£120-£150	$240-$300
Pluto's Quinpuplets				
Pluto	4½	c1937	£300	$600-$
Snow White and the 7 Dwarfs				
Bashful	3¼x1½	1981-1986	£80-£100	$160-$200
Bashful	3¾	1938	£150-£200	$300-$400
Doc	3x1¾	1981-1986	£125-£150	$500-$300
Doc	4	1938	£150-£200	$300-£400
Dopey	3¼x1¾	1981-1986	£80-£100	$160-$200
Dopey	3¾	1938	£150-£200	$300-$400
Grumpy	3x1¾	1981-1986	£80-£100	$160-$200
Grumpy	3½	1938	£150-£200	$300-$400
Happy	3¼x1½	1981-1986	£80-£100	$160-$200
Happy	4	1938	£150-£200	$300-$400
Sleepy	3x1½	1981-1986	£80-£100	$160-$200
Sleepy	4	1938	£150-£200	$300-$400
Sneezy	3¼x1½	1981-1986	£80-£100	$160-$200
Sneezy	3¾	1938	£150-£200	$300-$400
Snow White	3¾x4¾	1981-1986	£80-£100	$160-$200
Snow White	6⅜	1938	£150-£200	$300-$400
TV Pet Series				
Bengo	2⅜	1959	£25-£30	$50-$60
Bruno Jnr	2½	1961	£30-£35	$60-$70
Chee-Chee	2¼	1959	£20-£25	$40-$50
Droopy Jnr	2¼	1961	£35-£40	$70-$80
Fifi	2⅝	1959	£20-£25	$40-$50
Mitzi	2	1959	£25-£30	$50-$60
Pepi	2⅛	1959	£25-£30	$50-$60
Percy	1½	1965	£30-£35	$60-$70
Simon	2⅜	1959	£20-£30	$40-$60
Whisky	2	1965	£60-£70	$120-$140
Tom & Jerry				
Jerry	1⅞x1⅛	1973-1979	£35-£40	$70-$80
Tom	3⅝x2⅛	1973-1979	£35-£40	$70-$80

Figurines

Up until the late 1920s, George Wade & Son concentrated on industrial ceramics, but the need to diversify, and with the newly introduced cellulose finishing, it inspired the head designer, Jessie Van Hallen to produce well over 60 different models (some in different sizes as well) of human figurines. These were in production for about a decade, but production ceased when they found

Name	Size	Production	Market Price	

that the cellulose was unstable, it turning yellow and then peeled off. The moulds were used later for porcelain figures indicated by *.

Name	Size	Production	Market Price	
Alice	5½	1927-1937	£280-£320	$560-$640
Anita	6¾	1927-1937	£150-£250	$300-$500
Anita*	6¾	1935-1939	£350-£550	$700-$1100
Anna		1927-1937	£400-£600	$800-$1200
Anton	5¾	1927-1937	£180-£200	$360-$400
Anton	5¾	1927-1937	£250-£600	$500-$1200
Argentina	9½	1927-1937	£350-£550	$700-$1100
Babs*		1927-1937	£200-£300	$400-$600
Barbara	8½	1927-1937	£180-£220	$360-$440
Betty	5	1927-1937	£80-£120	$160-$240
Betty*	5	1935-1939	£350-£550	$700-$1100
Blossoms	7¾	1927-1937	£350-£550	$700-$1100
Blynken (prototype)	2⅛	1930s	£200-£400	$400-$800
Bride	7½	1927-1937	£140-£180	$280-$360
Carmen	9¼	1927-1937	£250-£400	$500-$800
Carnival	7	1927-1937	£180-£200	$360-$400
Carole	8½	1927-1937	£250-£400	$500-$800
Cherry	10	1927-1937	£250-£400	$500-$800
Choir Boy*	7⅜	1935-1939	£350-£550	$700-$1100
Christina	11	1927-1937	£200-£400	$400-$800
Claude	7¾	1927-1937	£150-£250	$300-$500
Colarado	10	1927-1937	£300-£400	$600-$800
Conchita	8¾	1927-1937	£250-£400	$500-$800
Curls	6	1927-1937	£180-£200	$360-$400
Curtsey	5	1927-1937	£80-£100	$160-$200
Curtsey*	5	1935-1939	£350-£550	$700-$1100
Cynthia	5	1927-1937	£100-£150	$200-$300
Cynthia*	5	1935-1939	£350-£550	$700-$1100
Daisette	10	1927-1937	£350-£550	$700-$1100
Dawn	8¼	1927-1937	£350-£550	$700-$1100
Delight	3	1927-1937	£180-£220	$360-$440
Dolly Vardon		1927-1937	£350-£550	$700-$1100
Elf	4	1927-1937	£180-£220	$360-$440
Ginger	9½	1927-1937	£350-£550	$700-$1100
Gloria	5¾	1927-1937	£180-£200	$360-$400
Grace	9¼	1927-1937	£250-£400	$500-$800
Grace*	9¼	1935-1939	£350-£550	$700-$1100
Greta	8	1927-1937	£250-£400	$500-$800
HRH Princess Elizabeth	5¾	1927-1937	£200-£300	$400-$600
Harriet	8	1927-1937	£150-£180	$300-$360
Helga	10	1927-1937	£150-£180	$300-$360
Hiawatha	4	1927-1937	£180-£220	$360-$440
Hille Bobbe	10	1927-1937	£200-£400	$400-$800

Name	Size	Production	Market Price	
Humoresque	8¼	1927-1937	£150-£180	$300-$360
Jean	6¾	1927-1937	£180-£200	$360-$400
Jeanette	6½	1927-1937	£150-£250	$300-$500
José	4½	1927-1937	£80-£100	$160-$200
José*	4½	1935-1939	£350-£550	$700-$1100
Joy	9¼	1927-1937	£300-£500	$600-$1000
Joy*	9¼	1935-1939	£250-£400	$500-$800
Joyce	7¼	1927-1937	£130-£160	$260-$320
Juliette*	9¼	1935-1939	£400-£600	$800-1200
June	7	1927-1937	£180-£200	$360-$400
Lotus	9¾	1927-1937	£150-£200	$300-$400
Madonna with Child	13½	1927-1937	£400-£600	$800-$1200
Madonna with Child*	13½	1935-1939	£700-£1100	$1400-$2200
Maria Theresa	8	1927-1937	£200-£250	$400-$500
Mimi	7¾	1927-1937	£150-£250	$300-$500
Old Nanny	9	1927-1937	£250-£350	$500-$700
Old Nanny*	9	1935-1939	£350-£550	$700-$1100
Pavlova	4½	1927-1937	£100-£120	$200-$240
Pavlova	9¼	1927-1937	£180-£220	$360-$440
Pavlova*	4½	1935-1939	£350-£550	$700-$1100
Peggy	6¾	1927-1937	£130-£160	$260-$320
Phyllis*	5¼	1927-1937	£250-£450	$500-$900
Pompadour	6	1927-1937	£120-£150	$240-$300
Queenie	4	1927-1937	£100-£150	$200-$300
Queenie*	3⅝	1935-1939	£350-£550	$700-$1100
Rhythm	9¾	1927-1937	£250-£350	$500-$700
Romance	6	1927-1937	£60-£90	$120-$180
Romance*	6½	1935-1939	£400-£600	$800-$1200
Sadie	13½	1927-1937	£250-£400	$500-$800
Springtime	9	1927-1937	£250-£400	$500-$800
Strawberry Girl	5¼	1927-1937	£120-£150	$240-$300
Sunshine	6½	1927-1937	£80-£100	$160-$200
Sunshine*	6½	1935-1939	£350-£550	$700-$1100
Swan Princess*	8¼	1930s	£400-£600	$800-$1200
Sylvia	7½	1927-1937	£150-£180	$300-$360
Tessa	5	1927-1937	£100-£120	$200-$240
Tony	4½	1927-1937	£100-£150	$200-$300
Winken (prototype)	2¾	1930s	£200-£400	$400-$800
Zena	8⅞	1927-1937	£250-£350	$500-$700
Zena	4	1927-1937	£120-£150	$240-$300
Zena*	4	1935-1939	£350-£550	$700-$1100
Zena*	8⅞	1935-1939	£450-£650	$900-$1300
British Characters				
Fishmonger	3⅛x1	1959	£120-£150	$240-$300
Lawyer	2⅞x1	1959	£120-£150	$240-$300
Pearly King	2¾x1	1959	£90-£120	$180-$240

Name	Size	Production	Market Price	
Pearly Queen	$2^7/_8$x$1^1/_2$	1959	£90-£120	$180-$240
Child Studies				
Boy				
English Costume				
decorated	$4^3/_4$	1962	£300-£500	$600-$1000
Scottish Costume				
decorated	$4^3/_4$	1962	£300-£500	$600-$1000
undecorated	$4^3/_4$	1962	£300-£500	$600-$1000
Girl				
Irish Costume				
decorated	$4^1/_2$	1962	£300-£500	$600-$1000
undecorated	$4^1/_2$	1962	£250-£350	$500-$700
Welsh Costume				
decorated	$5^1/_4$	1962	£300-£500	$600-$1000
Irish Character Figures				
Danny Boy	4	1990s	£15-£20	$30-$40
Phil the Fluter	$3^3/_4$	1990s	£30-£40	$60-$80
Kathleen	$3^1/_2$	1990s	£15-£20	$30-$40
Mother McCree	$2^1/_2$	1990s	£10-£15	$20-$30
Paddy McGinty	$3^1/_4$	1990s	£15-£20	$30-$40
Molly Malone	$3^1/_4$	1990s	£25-£35	$50-$70
Eileen Oge	$3^3/_4$	1990s	£15-£20	$30-$40
Paddy Reilly	$3^3/_4$	1990s	£25-£35	$50-$70
Rose of Tralee	4	1990s	£15-£20	$30-$40
Irish Songs Figures				
The Bard of Armagh	$5^1/_8$	1962-1986	£250-£350	$500-$700
Widda Cafferty	$6^1/_4$	1962-1986	£250-£350	$500-$700
Mother McCree	$8^1/_4$	1962-1986	£200-£300	$400-$600
Dan Murphy	$8^1/_4$	1962-1986	£200-£300	$400-$600
Eileen Oge	8	1962-1986	£200-£300	$400-$600
Baby	$4^1/_4$	1962-1986	£200-£300	$400-$600
Phil the Fluter		1962-1986	£200-£250	$400-$500
Little Crooked Paddy		1962-1986	£250-£350	$500-$700
The Star of County Down		1962-1986	£250-£350	$500-$700
The Irish Emigrant		1962-1986	£200-£300	$400-$600
Molly Malone		1962-1986	£250-£350	$500-$700
Mizky Mulligan		1962-1986	£250-£350	$500-$700
My Fair Ladies				
Caroline	$3^7/_8$	1990-1992	£20-£40	$40-$80
Hannah	$3^3/_4$	1990-1992	£20-£40	$40-$80
Kate	$3^7/_8$	1990-1992	£20-£40	$40-$80
Lisa	$3^3/_4$	1990-1992	£20-£40	$40-$80
Marie	$3^3/_4$	1990-1992	£20-£40	$40-$80
Rachel	$3^7/_8$	1990-1992	£20-£40	$40-$80
Rebecca	$3^7/_8$	1990-1992	£20-£40	$40-$80
Sarah	$3^3/_4$	1990-1992	£20-£40	$40-$80

Name	Size	Production	Market Price	
Amanda	4	1991-1992	£20-£40	$40-$80
Anita	3³/₄	1991-1992	£20-£40	$40-$80
Belinda	3³/₄	1991-1992	£20-£40	$40-$80
Diane	3³/₄	1991-1992	£20-£40	$40-$80
Emma	4	1991-1992	£20-£40	$40-$80
Lucy	3³/₄	1991-1992	£20-£40	$40-$80
Melissa	4	1991-1992	£20-£40	$40-$80
Natalie	4	1991-1992	£20-£40	$40-$80
Pageant				
King Henry VIII (cellulose)	4¹/₂	1927-1937	£400-£700	$800-$1400
Queen Elizabeth (cellulose)	4³/₈		£400-£700	$800-$1400
(There are six other figurines in this group)				
Knight Templar	9⁵/₈	1991	£200-£250	$400-$500
Sophisticated Ladies				
Emily	5³/₄	1991-1992	£70-£80	$140-$160
Felicity	6	1991-1992	£70-£80	$140-$160
Roxanne	5³/₄	1991-1992	£70-£80	$140-$160
Susannah	6	1991-1992	£70-£80	$140-$160

Mabel Lucie Attwell

Mabel Lucie Attwell was a popular illustrator, who created young children who had chubby rosy cheeks, blue eyes, plump stomachs and stubby legs. Her work appeared in countless magazines, books and postcards during the late 1950s and early 1960s. The set comprises a boy and a girl, both walking a dog on a lead and were designed by Paul Zalman. The original cost of the figures was six shillings and eleven pence (£0.35/$0.70).

Sam	3¹/₈x3	1959	£120-£180	$240-$360
Sarah	3x4	1959	£120-£180	$240-$360

Miscellaneous

Bisto Kids condiment set	4	mid 1970s	£125-£150	$250-$300
Zoo Lights				
Camel	1³/₄x1³/₄	1959	£10-£20	$20-$40
Husky	1³/₄x1³/₄	1959	£10-£20	$20-$40
West Highland Terrier	1³/₄x1³/₄	1959	£10-£20	$20-$40
Baby Polar Bear	1³/₄x1³/₄	1959	£10-£20	$20-$40
Baby Polar Bear	1³/₄x1³/₄	1959	£10-£20	$20-$40
Corgi	1³/₄x1³/₄	1959	£10-£20	$20-$40
Hare	1³/₄x1³/₄	1959	£10-£20	$20-$40
Llama	1³/₄x1³/₄	1959	£10-£20	$20-$40
Boxer	1³/₄x1³/₄	1959	£10-£20	$20-$40
Snowy Owl	1³/₄x1³/₄	1959	£10-£20	$20-$40

Novelty Animals and Birds

Name	Size	Production	Market Price	
Bernie & Poo	2	1955-1960	£60-£90	$120-$180
Dustbin Cat	1³/₄	1955-1960	£60-£90	$120-$180
Jonah and the Whale	1¹/₂	1955-1960	£60-£90	$120-$180
Jumbo Jim	1³/₄	1955-1960	£100-£150	$200-$300
Kitten on the Keys	1¹/₈	1955-1960	£100-£150	$200-$300
Drum Box				
Clara	2	1956-1959	£30-£50	$60-$100
Dora	2	1956-1959	£70-£90	$140-$180
Harpy	2	1956-1959	£30-£50	$60-$100
Jem	2	1956-1959	£30-£50	$60-$100
Trunky	2	1956-1959	£30-£50	$60-$100
Happy Families				
Giraffe (Baby)	⁵/₈x1¹/₄	1962-1965	£10-£15	$20-$30
Giraffe (Baby)	1⁹/₁₆x1	1962-1965	£15-£25	$30-$50
Giraffe (Parent)	2⁵/₁₆x1¹/₂	1962-1965	£15-£25	$30-$50
Hippo (Adult)	1¹/₈x2	1962-1965	£15-£25	$30-$50
Hippo (Baby)	⁵/₈x³/₄	1962-1965	£10-£15	$20-$30
Hippo (Baby)	1x³/₄	1962-1965	£15-£25	$30-$50
Mouse (Adult)	2x1	1962-1965	£15-£25	$30-$50
Mouse (Baby)	1x1	1962-1965	£15-£25	$30-$50
Mouse (Baby)	1¹/₁₆x1¹/₁₆	1962-1965	£15-£25	$30-$50
Rabbit (Baby)	1¹/₈x⁷/₈	1962-1965	£10-£15	$20-$30
Rabbit (Baby)	1¹/₄x1	1962-1965	£15-£25	$30-$50
Rabbit (Parent)	2x1	1962-1965	£15-£25	$30-$50
Tiger (Adult)	1⁹/₁₆x1⁹/₁₆	1962-1965	£100-£110	$200-$220
Tiger (Baby)	³/₈x1³/₁₆	1962-1965	£100-£110	$200-$220
Tiger (Baby)	³/₈x1³/₁₆	1962-1965	£100-£110	$200-$220
Cat (Adult)	1⁷/₈x1¹/₄	1978-1986	£15-£25	$30-$50
Cat (Kitten)	1¹/₄x1¹/₄	1978-1986	£10-£15	$20-$30
Cat (Kitten)	1³/₈x³/₄	1978-1986	£10-£15	$20-$30
Dog (Adult)	2x1¹/₂	1978-1986	£15-£25	$30-$50
Dog (Puppy)	1¹/₄x1³/₈	1978-1986	£15-£25	$30-$50
Dog (Puppy)	1¹/₄x1¹/₈	1978-1986	£15-£25	$30-$50
Elephant (Adult)	1¹/₈x1¹/₈	1978-1986	£15-£25	$30-$50
Elephant (Baby)	1³/₄x⁷/₈	1978-1986	£10-£15	$20-$30
Elephant (Baby)	1x⁷/₈	1978-1986	£10-£15	$20-$30
Frog (Adult)	⁷/₈x1⁹/₁₆	1978-1986	£15-£25	$30-$50
Frog (Baby)	⁵/₈x1³/₈	1978-1986	£15-£25	$30-$50
Frog (Baby)	1x⁷/₈	1978-1986	£15-£25	$30-$50
Giraffe (Adult)	2⁵/₁₆x1¹/₂	1978-1986	£15-£25	$30-$50
Giraffe (Baby)	⁵/₈x1¹/₄	1978-1986	£15-£25	$30-$50
Giraffe (Baby)	1⁹/₁₆x1	1978-1986	£15-£25	$30-$50
Hippo (Adult)	1¹/₈x1¹/₈	1978-1986	£15-£25	$30-$50
Hippo (Baby)	⁵/₈x³/₄	1978-1986	£15-£25	$30-$50

Name	Size	Production	Market Price	
Hippo (Baby)	1x³/₄	1978-1986	£15-£25	$30-$50
Mouse (Adult)	2x1	1978-1986	£15-£25	$30-$50
Mouse (Baby)	1x1	1978-1986	£10-£15	$20-$30
Mouse (Baby)	1¹/₁₆x1¹/₁₆	1978-1986	£10-£15	$20-$30
Owl (Baby)	1x³/₄	1978-1986	£15-£25	$30-$50
Owl (Baby)	⁷/₈x⁵/₈	1978-1986	£15-£25	$30-$50
Owl (Parent)	1³/₄x³/₄	1978-1986	£15-£25	$30-$50
Pig (Adult)	1¹/₈x1¹/₈	1978-1986	£15-£25	$30-$50
Pig (Baby)	⁵/₈x³/₄	1978-1986	£15-£25	$30-$50
Pig (Baby)	⁹/₁₆x1⁵/₈	1978-1986	£15-£25	$30-$50
Rabbit (Baby)	1¹/₈x⁷/₈	1978-1986	£15-£25	$30-$50
Rabbit (Parent)	2x1	1978-1986	£15-£25	$30-$50
Rabbit (Parent)	1¹/₄x1	1978-1986	£15-£25	$30-$50
Set A				
Minikins	1¹/₄x1¹/₄	1956	£10-£15	$20-$30
Set B				
Minikins	1¹/₄x1¹/₄	1957	£10-£15	$20-$30
Set C				
Minikins	1¹/₈x⁷/₈	1958	£10-£15	$20-$30
Treasures				
The Elephant Chain		1956	£350-£550	$700-$1100

Premium & Promotion

Probably the most common way that anyone starts a collection. Receiving a free gift with any product has always been a popular gimmick with manufacturers, especially if it is of popular appeal and fairly high quality, that you will want to acquire the set. George Wade & Son Ltd decided in the mid 1960s to enter this up and coming lucrative market, and began with about 20 different models. By 1968 this had increased to well over 40, and it was from this that Red Rose Tea made by Brooke Bond Foods of Canada, chose 32 to form a promotion. This proved so successful, that Wade added another 28 figures and sold them retail under the trade name of Whimsies. Of the original 32 models, seven were never included in the retail range, (Frog – same mould as Bull Frog Whimsie but was coloured green/yellow – Butterfly, Poodle, Seal, Angel Fish, Terrapin and Alligator).

Miscellaneous

Name	Size	Production	Market Price	
Black Zebra	1⁵/₈x1³/₈	mid 1960s	£20-£30	$40-$60
Bronti	1x1¹/₂	mid 1960s	£5-£10	$10-$20
Brown Bear	1⁵/₈x1	mid 1960s	£25-£75	$50-$150
Dino	1³/₈x1³/₈	mid 1960s	£5-£10	$10-$20
Friar Tuck	1³/₄	1989-1990	£20-£30	$40-$60
Maid Marian	2⁵/₈	1989-1990	£20-£30	$40-$60
Rhino	1x1⁵/₈	mid 1960s	£5-£10	$10-$20
Robin Hood	2³/₄	1989-1990	£20-£30	$40-$60

Name	Size	Production	Market Price	
Tiger	$1\frac{1}{2}$x1	mid 1960s	£5-£10	$10-$20
Red Rose Tea				
Old King Cole	$1\frac{1}{2}$x1	1971-1979	£10-£15	$20-$30
Little Jack Horner	$1\frac{3}{8}$x1	1971-1979	£5-£10	$10-$20
Humpty Dumpty	$1\frac{1}{2}$x$\frac{7}{8}$	1971-1979	£5-£10	$10-$20
Jack	$1\frac{1}{4}$x$1\frac{1}{4}$	1971-1979	£10-£15	$20-$30
Jill	$1\frac{1}{8}$x$1\frac{1}{4}$	1971-1979	£10-£15	$20-$30
Tom the Piper's Son	$1\frac{5}{8}$x$1\frac{3}{8}$	1971-1979	£10-£15	$20-$30
Little Boy Blue	$1\frac{5}{8}$x1	1971-1979	£10-£15	$20-$30
Little Miss Muffet	$1\frac{1}{2}$x$1\frac{3}{8}$	1971-1979	£15-£20	$30-$40
Pied Piper	$1\frac{3}{4}$x$1\frac{1}{8}$	1971-1979	£10-£15	$20-$30
Doctor Foster	$1\frac{3}{4}$x$\frac{7}{8}$	1971-1979	£15-£20	$30-$40
Mother Goose	$1\frac{5}{8}$x$1\frac{1}{4}$	1971-1979	£20-£25	$40-$50
Old Woman Who Lived Lived in a Shoe	$1\frac{3}{8}$x$1\frac{5}{8}$	1971-1979	£10-£15	$20-$30
Goosey Gander	$1\frac{3}{8}$x1	1971-1979	£10-£15	$20-$30
Wee Willie Winkie	$1\frac{3}{4}$x1	1971-1979	£10-£15	$20-$30
Little Bo Peep	$1\frac{3}{4}$x$\frac{3}{4}$	1971-1979	£10-£15	$20-$30
Three Bears	$1\frac{3}{8}$x$1\frac{1}{2}$	1971-1979	£20-£25	$40-$50
Puss In Boots	$1\frac{3}{4}$x$\frac{3}{4}$	1971-1979	£15-£20	$30-$40
The House That Jack Built	$1\frac{1}{4}$x$1\frac{1}{4}$	1971-1979	£15-£20	$30-$40
Little Red Riding Hood	$1\frac{3}{4}$x$\frac{7}{8}$	1971-1979	£10-£15	$20-$30
Queen of Hearts				
– Two large hearts	$1\frac{3}{4}$x1	1971-1979	£20-£25	$40-$50
– Two small hearts	$1\frac{3}{4}$x1	1971-1979	£20-£25	$40-$50
– Multi-hearts	$1\frac{3}{4}$x1	1971-1979	£25-£35	$50-$70
Baa Baa Black Sheep	$\frac{7}{8}$x$1\frac{1}{8}$	1971-1979	£15-£20	$30-$40
Hickory Dickory Dock	$1\frac{3}{4}$x$\frac{3}{4}$	1971-1979	£10-£15	$20-$30
Gingerbread Man	$1\frac{5}{8}$x$1\frac{1}{16}$	1971-1979	£25-£35	$50-$70
Cat and the Fiddle	$1\frac{7}{8}$x1	1971-1979	£5-£20	$10-$40
Frog	$\frac{7}{8}$x$\frac{1}{8}$	1967-1973	£3-£6	$6-$12
Butterfly	$\frac{1}{2}$x$1\frac{3}{4}$	1967-1973	£3-£6	$6-$12
Poodle	$1\frac{5}{8}$x$1\frac{5}{8}$	1967-1973	£3-£6	$6-$12
Seal	$1\frac{1}{2}$x$1\frac{1}{4}$	1967-1973	£3-£6	$6-$12
Angel Fish	$1\frac{1}{4}$x$1\frac{3}{8}$	1967-1973	£3-£6	$6-$12
Terrapin	$\frac{3}{8}$x$1\frac{5}{8}$	1967-1973	£3-£6	$6-$12
Alligator	$\frac{1}{2}$x$1\frac{1}{2}$	1967-1973	£3-£6	$6-$12
Robertsons Gollies				
Accordian Player	$2\frac{5}{8}$	1960s	£120-£150	$240-$300
Clarinet Player	$2\frac{5}{8}$	1960s	£120-£150	$240-$300
Double Bass Player	$2\frac{5}{8}$	1960s	£120-£150	$240-$300
Saxophone Player	$2\frac{5}{8}$	1960s	£120-£150	$240-$300
Trumpet Player	$2\frac{5}{8}$	1960s	£120-£150	$240-$300
Slimbridge Wildfowl Trust				
Ruddy Duck (ltd ed 3400)	$1\frac{3}{8}$	1976	£150-£200	$300-$400

Name	Size	Production	Market Price	

Snippets
Set 1

Name	Size	Production	Market Price	
The Mayflower	2¼x1½	1956-1958	£40-£60	$80-$120
The Revenge	2¼x1½	1956-1959	£40-£60	$80-$120
The Santa Maria	2¼x1½	1956-1959	£40-£60	$80-$120

Set 2

Bear	2¼x1½	1956-1959	£150-£200	$300-$400
Gretel	2¼x1½	1956-1959	£90-£110	$180-$220
Hansel	2¼x1½	1956-1959	£90-£110	$180-$220

Wade Collectables

Welcome Home	3¾x4¾	1993-1996	£25-£35	$50-$70
Togetherness	3¾x4¾	1993-1996	£25-£35	$50-$70
Fireside Friend	3¾x4¾	1993-1996	£25-£35	$50-$70
Snow man	5	1994	£40-£50	$80-$100
Snow woman	4⅞	1995	£30-£40	$60-$80
Snow children		1996	£20-£30	$40-$60

Wall Masks

Dyllis		1927-1937	£300-£500	$600-$1000
Frolic		1927-1937	£300-£500	$600-$1000
Pan		1927-1937	£300-£500	$600-$1000
Sonia		1927-1937	£300-£500	$600-$1000

Whimsie-Land

English Wildlife

Field Mouse	1¼x1½	1987	£20-£25	$40-$50
Golden Eagle	1⅜x1¾	1987	£15-£20	$30-$40
Otter	1½x1⅝	1987	£10-£15	$20-$30
Partridge	1½x1¾	1987	£10-£15	$20-$30
Pheasant	1¼x2	1987	£20-£25	$40-$50

Farmyard

Cow	1¼x1¼	1985	£10-£15	$20-$30
Duck	1⅝x1	1985	£10-£15	$20-$30
Goat	1¼x1⅛	1985	£10-£15	$20-$30
Pig	1⅛x1⅛	1985	£10-£15	$20-$30
Rooster	2x1⅛	1985	£10-£15	$20-$30

Hedgerow

Badger	1x1⅜	1986	£10-£15	$20-$30
Fox	1⅜x1¼	1986	£15-£25	$30-$50
Hedgehog	⅞x1¼	1986	£10-£15	$20-$30
Owl	1½x⅞	1986	£10-£15	$20-$30

Name	Size	Production	Market Price	
Squirrel	$1\frac{1}{2}$x$\frac{3}{4}$	1986	£10-£15	$20-$30
Pets				
Kitten	1x$1\frac{5}{8}$	1984	£10-£15	$20-$30
Pony	$1\frac{1}{2}$x$1\frac{1}{2}$	1984	£10-£15	$20-$30
Puppy	$1\frac{3}{8}$x$1\frac{3}{8}$	1984	£10-£15	$20-$30
Rabbit	2x$\frac{7}{8}$	1984	£10-£15	$20-$30
Retriever	$1\frac{1}{4}$x$1\frac{5}{8}$	1984	£10-£15	$20-$30
Wildlife				
Elephant	$1\frac{3}{8}$x$1\frac{3}{8}$	1984	£10-£15	$20-$30
Giraffe	2x$1\frac{1}{4}$	1984	£10-£15	$20-$30
Lion	$1\frac{1}{4}$x$1\frac{7}{8}$	1984	£10-£15	$20-$30
Panda	$1\frac{3}{8}$x$\frac{7}{8}$	1984	£10-£15	$20-$30
Tiger	$\frac{3}{4}$x$1\frac{3}{4}$	1984	£10-£15	$20-$30

Whimsies

Series 1

Set 1

Name	Size	Production	Market Price	
Horse	$1\frac{1}{2}$x$2\frac{1}{8}$	1953	£15-£25	$30-$50
Leaping Fawn	$1\frac{7}{8}$x$1\frac{1}{2}$	1953	£10-£20	$20-$40
Poodle	$1\frac{1}{2}$x$1\frac{3}{4}$	1953	£10-£20	$20-$40
Spaniel	1x$1\frac{3}{4}$	1953	£10-£20	$20-$40
Squirrel	$1\frac{1}{4}$x$1\frac{7}{8}$	1953	£10-£20	$20-$40

Set 2

Bull	$1\frac{3}{4}$x$2\frac{1}{8}$	1954	£30-£40	$60-$80
Dachshund	$1\frac{1}{8}$x$1\frac{1}{2}$	1954	£30-£40	$60-$80
Hare	$1\frac{1}{8}$x$1\frac{3}{4}$	1954	£10-£20	$20-$40
Kitten	$1\frac{3}{8}$x$1\frac{3}{4}$	1954	£20-£40	$40-$80
Lamb	$1\frac{7}{8}$x$1\frac{1}{4}$	1954	£20-£30	$40-$60

Set 3

Badger	$1\frac{1}{4}$x2	1955	£10-£20	$20-$40
Fox Cub	$1\frac{3}{8}$x$1\frac{5}{8}$	1955	£20-£40	$40-$80
Retriever	$1\frac{1}{4}$x$1\frac{7}{8}$	1955	£15-£25	$30-$50
Shetland Pony	$1\frac{3}{8}$x2	1955	£10-£20	$20-$40
Stoat	$1\frac{1}{8}$x$1\frac{3}{4}$	1955	£20-£30	$40-$60

Set 4

Baby Elephant	$1\frac{1}{4}$x$1\frac{7}{8}$	1955	£15-£25	$30-$50
Crocodile	$\frac{3}{4}$x$1\frac{5}{8}$	1955	£20-£30	$40-$60
Lion	$1\frac{1}{4}$x$1\frac{5}{8}$	1955	£20-£30	$40-$60
Monkey	$1\frac{7}{8}$x$1\frac{5}{8}$	1955	£10-£20	$20-$40
Rhinoceros	$1\frac{3}{4}$x$2\frac{3}{8}$	1955	£10-£20	$20-$40

Set 5

Beagle	$\frac{3}{4}$x1	1956	£25-£30	$50-$60
Colt	$1\frac{7}{16}$x$1\frac{1}{8}$	1956	£15-£25	$30-$50
Foal	$1\frac{1}{4}$x$1\frac{3}{4}$	1956	£15-£25	$30-$50
Mare	$1\frac{7}{8}$x2	1956	£15-£25	$30-$50

Name	Size	Production	Market Price	
Set 6				
Baby Polar Bear	$\frac{7}{8}$x$1\frac{1}{8}$	1956	£10-£20	$20-$40
Baby Seal	$\frac{7}{8}$x$1\frac{1}{8}$	1956	£10-£20	$20-$40
Husky	$1\frac{1}{4}$x$1\frac{1}{8}$	1956	£10-£20	$20-$40
King Penguin	$1\frac{3}{16}$x$\frac{5}{8}$	1956	£10-£20	$20-$40
Polar Bear	$1\frac{3}{4}$x$1\frac{3}{4}$	1956	£10-£20	$20-$40
Set 7				
Alsatian	$1\frac{3}{8}$x$1\frac{5}{8}$	1957	£15-£25	$30-$50
Boxer	$1\frac{3}{8}$x$1\frac{1}{2}$	1957	£15-£25	$30-$50
Corgi	1x$1\frac{1}{4}$	1957	£15-£25	$30-$50
Saint Bernard	$1\frac{1}{2}$x$1\frac{7}{8}$	1957	£15-£25	$30-$50
West Highland Terrier	1x$1\frac{1}{4}$	1957	£15-£25	$30-$50
Set 8				
Bactrian Camel	$1\frac{1}{2}$x$1\frac{5}{8}$	1958	£10-£20	$20-$40
Cockatoo	$1\frac{1}{8}$x$1\frac{1}{4}$	1958	£15-£20	$30-$40
Giant Panda	$1\frac{1}{2}$x1	1958	£10-£20	$20-$40
Lion Cub	1x1	1958	£10-£20	$20-$40
Llama	$1\frac{3}{4}$x$1\frac{1}{8}$	1958	£10-£20	$20-$40
Set 9				
Bear Cub	$1\frac{1}{8}$x$1\frac{1}{8}$	1958	£10-£20	$20-$40
Cougar	$\frac{3}{4}$x$1\frac{7}{8}$	1958	£15-£25	$30-$50
Grizzly Bear	$1\frac{7}{8}$x$\frac{7}{8}$	1958	£15-£25	$30-$50
Racoon	$1\frac{1}{8}$x$1\frac{1}{8}$	1958	£10-£20	$20-$40
Snowy Owl	$1\frac{1}{8}$x$1\frac{3}{16}$	1958	£20-£30	$40-$60
Set 10				
Foxhound	1x$1\frac{3}{4}$	1959	£30-£40	$40-$80
Italian Goat	$1\frac{3}{8}$x$1\frac{1}{2}$	1959	£30-£40	$40-$80
Piglet	$\frac{7}{8}$x$1\frac{1}{2}$	1959	£20-£30	$40-$60
Shire Horse	2x$2\frac{1}{2}$	1959	£100-£110	$200-$220
Shire Horse (brown glaze)	2x$2\frac{1}{8}$	1959	£200-£220	$400-$440
Swan	$\frac{7}{8}$x$1\frac{1}{2}$	1959	£50-£100	$100-$200
Series 2				
Set 1				
Fawn	$1\frac{3}{8}$x$1\frac{1}{4}$	1971-1984	£2-£5	$4-$10
Kitten	$1\frac{3}{8}$x$1\frac{3}{8}$	1971-1984	£2-£5	$4-$10
Mongrel	$1\frac{1}{8}$x$1\frac{1}{2}$	1971-1984	£2-£5	$4-$10
Rabbit	$1\frac{1}{8}$x$1\frac{7}{8}$	1971-1984	£5-£8	$10-$16
Spaniel	$1\frac{3}{8}$x$1\frac{3}{8}$	1971-1984	£2-£5	$4-$10
Set 2				
Beaver	$1\frac{1}{4}$x$1\frac{1}{4}$	1972-1984	£2-£5	$4-$10
Bushbaby	$1\frac{1}{4}$x$1\frac{1}{8}$	1972-1984	£2-£5	$4-$10
Corgi	$1\frac{1}{2}$x$1\frac{1}{2}$	1972-1984	£2-£5	$4-$10
Duck	$1\frac{1}{4}$x$1\frac{1}{2}$	1972-1984	£2-£5	$4-$10
Fox	$1\frac{3}{8}$x$1\frac{1}{2}$	1972-1984	£2-£5	$4-$10
Set 3				
Bear Cub	$1\frac{3}{8}$x$\frac{7}{8}$	1972-1984	£2-£5	$4-$10

Name	Size	Production	Market Price	
Otter	$1^1/_4$x$1^1/_2$	1972-1984	£2-£5	$4-$10
Owl	$1^1/_2$x$^7/_8$	1972-1984	£2-£5	$4-$10
Setter	$1^3/_8$x$1^7/_8$	1972-1984	£2-£5	$4-$10
Trout	$1^1/_8$x$1^3/_8$	1972-1984	£2-£5	$4-$10
Set 4				
Chimp	$1^1/_2$x$1^3/_8$	1973-1984	£2-£5	$4-$10
Elephant	$1^3/_8$x$1^3/_4$	1973-1984	£2-£5	$4-$10
Giraffe	$1^1/_2$x$1^1/_2$	1973-1984	£2-£5	$4-$10
Hippo (large)	$1^1/_{16}$x$1^3/_4$	1973-1984	£2-£5	$4-$10
Hippo (small)	$^7/_8$x$1^1/_2$	1973-1984	£2-£5	$4-$10
Lion	$1^3/_8$x$1^3/_4$	1973-1984	£2-£5	$4-$10
Set 5				
Alsatian	$1^1/_4$x$1^7/_8$	1974-1984	£2-£5	$4-$10
Field Mouse	$1^1/_2$x$^3/_4$	1974-1984	£2-£5	$4-$10
Hedgehog	$^7/_8$x$1^3/_4$	1974-1984	£2-£5	$4-$10
Pinemarten	$1^3/_8$x$1^1/_2$	1974-1984	£2-£5	$4-$10
Squirrel	$1^3/_8$x$1^3/_8$	1974-1984	£2-£5	$4-$10
Set 6				
Collie	$1^1/_4$x$1^3/_8$	1975-1984	£2-£5	$4-$10
Cow	$1^1/_4$x$1^1/_2$	1975-1984	£2-£5	$4-$10
Horse	$1^5/_8$x$1^3/_8$	1975-1984	£2-£5	$4-$10
Lamb	$1^3/_8$x$1^1/_8$	1975-1984	£2-£5	$4-$10
Pig	$^5/_{16}$x$1^1/_2$	1975-1984	£2-£5	$4-$10
Set 7				
Camel	$1^3/_8$x$1^5/_8$	1976-1984	£2-£5	$4-$10
Gorilla	$1^1/_2$x$1^1/_4$	1976-1984	£2-£5	$4-$10
Leopard	$^7/_8$x$1^7/_8$	1976-1984	£2-£5	$4-$10
Rhino	$^7/_8$x$1^5/_8$	1976-1984	£2-£5	$4-$10
Zebra	$1^5/_8$x$1^1/_2$	1976-1984	£2-£5	$4-$10
Set 8				
Cat	$1^1/_2$x$^7/_8$	1977-1984	£2-£5	$4-$10
Donkey	$1^1/_4$x$1^5/_8$	1977-1984	£2-£5	$4-$10
Mouse	$1^1/_2$x1	1977-1984	£2-£5	$4-$10
Owl	$1^1/_2$x1	1977-1984	£2-£5	$4-$10
Ram	$1^3/_{16}$x$1^3/_8$	1977-1984	£2-£5	$4-$10
Set 9				
Angel Fish	$1^3/_8$x$1^1/_4$	1978-1984	£5-£10	$10-$20
Dolphin	$1^1/_8$x$1^3/_4$	1978-1984	£5-£10	$10-$20
Pelican	$1^3/_4$x$1^3/_8$	1978-1984	£2-£5	$4-$10
Seahorse	2x$^3/_4$	1978-1984	£2-£5	$4-$10
Turtle	$^9/_{16}$x2	1978-1984	£2-£5	$4-$10
Set 10				
Kangaroo	$1^5/_8$x$1^1/_8$	1979-1984	£2-£5	$4-$10
Koala Bear	$1^1/_8$x$1^1/_8$	1979-1984	£2-£5	$4-$10
Langur	$1^3/_8$x$1^1/_2$	1979-1984	£2-£5	$4-$10
Orangutan	$1^1/_4$x$1^1/_4$	1979-1984	£2-£5	$4-$10

Name	Size	Production	Market Price	
Tiger	1½x1⅛	1979-1984	£2-£5	$4-$10
Set 11				
Bison	1⅜x1¾	1979-1984	£2-£5	$4-$10
Bluebird	⅝x1½	1979-1984	£2-£5	$4-$10
Bullfrog	⅞x1	1979-1984	£2-£5	$4-$10
Raccoon	1x1½	1979-1984	£2-£5	$4-$10
Wild Boar	1⅛x1⅝	1979-1984	£2-£5	$4-$10
Set 12				
Husky	1⁷⁄₁₆x1⅛	1980-1984	£2-£5	$4-$10
Penguin	1⅝x¾	1980-1984	£5-£10	$10-$20
Polar Bear	1⅛x1⅝	1980-1984	£2-£5	$4-$10
Seal Pup	1x1½	1980-1984	£2-£5	$4-$10
Walrus	1¼x1¼	1980-1984	£2-£5	$4-$10

Whoppas

Whoppas were introduced in 1976 and although not exact copies of the Whimsies series, they were larger models on the same theme. The main reason they were introduced was to fill a gap in the product range between the Whimsies and Nursery Favourites.

Name	Size	Production	Market Price	
Set 1				
Brown Bear	1½x1¾	1976-1981	£5-£10	$10-$20
Elephant	2⅛x2	1976-1981	£5-£10	$10-$20
Hippo	1⅜x2⅛	1976-1981	£5-£10	$10-$20
Polar Bear	1½x2⅛	1976-1981	£5-£10	$10-$20
Tiger	1⅛x2½	1976-1981	£5-£10	$10-$20
Set 2				
Bison	1¾x2⅛	1977-1981	£5-£10	$10-$20
Bobcat	1½x1⅞	1977-1981	£5-£10	$10-$20
Chipmunk	2⅛x1	1977-1981	£5-£10	$10-$20
Racoon	1½x2¼	1977-1981	£5-£10	$10-$20
Wolf	2¼x1¾	1977-1981	£5-£10	$10-$20
Set 3				
Badger	1½x1⅞	1978-1981	£10-£20	$20-$40
Fox	1¼x2½	1978-1981	£10-£20	$20-$40
Hedgehog	1¼x1⅞	1978-1981	£10-£20	$20-$40
Otter	1¼x2	1978-1981	£10-£20	$20-$40
Stoat	1½x2⅛	1978-1981	£10-£20	$20-$40

Backstamps and Marks

As with most ceramic firms there are seemingly endless backstamps and types of marks used over the duration of the life of a pottery. What I have included here are the basic types you are most likely to come across. All or most of these will have variations in design. You will also find that there are various methods of making the marks with some marks using several methods, these can vary from the use of transfer prints, handpainting, impressed or stamping the marks into the body, moulded marks and rubber stamped ink marks. In the past ten years there has been a growing demand for personalised special backstamps often designed by the commissioning agents.

Wade & Co., Union Pottery, Burslem 1887-1927

Backstamp No 1

Backstamp No 2

George Wade & Son Ltd., Manchester Pottery, Burslem 1922–

Backstamp No 3
1930s. In red and/or
block printed

Backstamp No 4

Backstamp No 6
1950s-1980s

Backstamp No 5
Late 1940s

Wade Heath & Co., (Ltd.), High Street Works, 1927–

Backstamp No 8
Late 1930s

Backstamp No 7
1928-Late 1930s

Backstamp No 9
1940s-1950s

WADE ENGLAND

Backstamp No 10
1940s

Backstamp No 11
Late 1940s-1950s

Backstamp No 12
1953-1960s

Backstamp No 13
1950s

Backstamp No 14
1954 onwards

Backstamp No 15
1955 with year letter

Backstamp No 16
1970s

Backstamp No 17
Late 1970s

**Wade Ceramics
Limited,
1990–today**

Backstamp No 20

Backstamp No 21

Bibliography

The Wade Dynasty D. Lee, Kudos, 1996
The World of Wade Book 1 I. Warner and M. Posgay, Antique Publications, 1994
The World of Wade Book 2 I. Warner and M. Posgay, Antique Publications, 1994
Wade Price Trends, 1st edition The Glass Press Inc., 1996
Encyclopedia of British Pottery and Porcelain Marks G. Godden, Barrie & Jenkins, 1964
Charlton Standard Catalogue of Wade Pat Murray Volume 1, Charlton Press, 1996

The magazine of The Official International Wade Collectors Club
The Sentinel evening newspaper
The Antiques Trade Gazette
Kelly's Trade Directories
The Pottery Gazette & Glass Trades Review
The Pottery & Glass Record
Cox's Potteries Annual & Yearbook
The Antiques Bulletin

DRACULA!

Once again, Dracula, the Prince of Darkness has returned and this time it may very well be forever!!

This year NEXUS are proud to present the only fully endorsed and licensed, specially commissioned porcelain Dracula figurine to commemorate the centenary of Bram Stoker's chilling classic novel and the 40th anniversary of Hammer Horror, the film studio whom so vividly captured the essence of terror in their many horror films which included Dracula (1958) and many subsequent sequels.

This exclusively commissioned Nexus sculpture, in conjunction with the most collectable porcelain/ceramic companies in the UK – Wade Ceramics Ltd, is modelled on Christopher Lee's mesmerising portrayal of Count Dracula by the outstanding sculptural talent of Wade Ceramics Ltd's own Ken Holmes.

Standing at a height of 27cm (10½ins) each figure has been individually hand decorated in fine detail, right down to the 22 carat gold signet ring, and comes complete with its own wooden display stand, presentation box and certificate of authenticity. Each figure will also bear the Hammer Horror 40th Anniversary logo on the base. In addition the Nexus/Wade Dracula is issued in a strictly limited edition size of just 2,500 figures worldwide and will be available by mail order for just GB£90.00 (inc p&p). For more information about this officially licenced 1997 Dracula figurine, simply contact the relevant address below by fax or telephone as soon as possible.

This exclusive DRACULA sculpture is available in **two** distinct finishes, High Gloss Glaze (pictured above) and Satin/Matt. To order DRACULA please contact the following for further details and order form:

The Gloss version DRACULA – Ltd edition size 1250 worldwide is ONLY available from:
Nexus, 51 Brookthorpe Way, Silverdale Estate, Wilford, Nottingham NG11 7FE
Telephone: (44+) 0115 982 2047   Fax: (44+) 0115 982 2137

The Satin/Matt version DRACULA – Ltd edition size 1250 worldwide is ONLY available from:
The Official International Wade Collectors Club, Royal Works, Westport Road, Burslem, Stoke-on-Trent, Staffordshire ST6 4AP
Tel: (44+) 01782 588400   Fax: (44+) 01782 575195

PRICE: (UK) GB£90.00   (OVERSEAS) US$152.00

WADE AUCTIONS
AT PHILLIPS

*Phillips hold two Wade auctions a year
(usually May and October). We are pleased
to give advice for auction regarding
Wade pieces particularly rare
and unusual pieces.*

*For further information contact
Mark Oliver on 0171-468 8233*